# Stop Marketing.

# Be Remarkable!

### Mike Montano

This is a special pre-release of *Stop Marketing. Be Remarkable!* I appreciate any feedback you may have. Please enjoy. - Mike Montano (mike@smbrbook.com)

# Table of Contents

# Dedication

TO MY CHILDREN MICHAEL, MARIAH, VANESSA AND
SOPHIA,

My life's gifts.
My world has been driven to new levels of purpose and
inspiration because of you.
I love you. Thank you for always believing in me.

SUPPORT STRONGER HEALTHIER BABIES AND
MOTHERS

Ten percent of author proceeds are donated to March of
Dimes, a non-profit organization dedicated to funding
research to save babies' lives.

# Acknowledgements

First and foremost to Tia, my love, I cannot thank you enough for all your support, your inspiration and your encouragement. Your presence in my life has been a blessing. I truly appreciate you, not only for what you do but more importantly for who you are.

I also want to thank the most inspirational person in the world. At the young age of 79 you have a love of life so strong that you join your adrenalin-junkie friends for skydiving and bungee jumping excursions, just to name a few. Mom, you're my hero. I can only hope to follow your example and leave a legacy of hard work and extreme play. Your passion and hunger for life has led me to achieve results I never dreamed possible.

In addition, I want to thank my recently deceased father, Sergeant Mike Montano Sr. of the United States Marine Corps, who did what he knew best and taught me to be a fighter and planted a seed enabling me to handle all of life's adversities. Thank you Dad, for loving me so much that you gave me the ultimate gift a father can pass on to his son, the gift of preparing me for life.

I'd also like to thank my sister, Lisa, for looking after me as a kid and being someone I can always count on. Thank you for continuing to be an awesome and incredibly caring big sister.

Thank you to my friends and believers from very early on and always showed me love, trust and confidence right from the start. Thanks to one of my best friends on the planet, Kenny Chapman — you know you're my boy! To the early adopters; Jeff Belk, Tim Flynn, Matt Morse, Barry Kindt, Garrett Cook and Mike Agugliaro, who believed in me when others didn't, thank you!

My greatest fan: Lisa Schardt your support and love is overwhelming--Luv, luv, luv you! Susan Kimball who opened doors for me so early on, I am forever grateful. My Corner Men, Joel Mejia and Javier Vidrio that no matter how many life beat downs and financial lows of lows we have endured and overcome, you have always remained loyal and at my side.

To my monthly success team of John Bell, Jim Hernandez, Bret Dudl, Andrew Felsburg, Glen Minteer, Jeff Dechamplain, Steve Klein, David Park and Allen Honadle, thank you for holding me accountable to higher standards in every aspect of my life.

To all current and future members of ReviewBuzz who share the uncommon belief that being remarkable is essential to being successful in both business and in life. Thank you for your support, I wish you and your businesses all the prosperity in the world.

Tony Hsieh, your remarkable story has inspired me to take massive action and focus on my passion. Your approach to business is truly incredible and what I admire most is you continue to practice what you preach; leading by example. Thank so very much for your inspiration and continued commitment to following your life's purpose of delivering happiness.

One of the greatest experiences I've ever had was being exposed to Tony Robbins' seminar, *Unleash the Power Within*. It was an event that forever changed my life. Learning the power of a simple incantation opened the door to opportunities I had never previously considered. I am forever a fan and am indebted to your powerful seminars for changing my life. Finishing this book is just one of the many dreams you inspired me to pursue. In all your teachings you helped me make the seemingly impossible, possible.

Thank you to Christine Messier, my collaborative editor at Your Voice, Inc., for her commitment to excellence and for sharing her expertise in guiding me through this process.

And last but certainly not least, very special thanks for the daily support from my team: Rick, Satu, Ruby, Ramon, David, Joni, Shanelle, Kim, Jill, Susan and Seth. I appreciate you all like family.

# Introduction: My Life as a Closet Internet Market

Like some of you reading this book I started my career with less than an encouraging start. Unexpected pitfalls and some incredible obstacles found their way in the middle of my path which made everything feel like an uphill battle.

I was 23 years old with a family of five and a brand new business in the home services industry. I attended a business learning conference and after listening to many incredible speakers I bravely and enthusiastically approached one for some advice. He looked me up and down with an expression of disapproval and said "why don't you start with buying a Sawzall" (A common tool used by new construction plumbers) and turned his back on me. Well, there it was; the judgment that I was too young, too inexperienced and flat out foolish.

In almost every way he was right. I was young and only able to work on my new business part time because of my full-time new construction job. Being the son of a Marine I wasn't discouraged in the least. Although I was young I had two years of business school and had been running many of my enterprises since I was nine years old. I was motivated to support my family and create a successful business and I was certainly not going to let my inexperience slow me down.

I lacked resources so I found creative ways to adjust. I started by taking the doors off my bedroom closet because there was no other space to set up a desk when the five of us were sharing an 800-square-foot apartment. So there I sat working and planning out the business amongst my tie and belt rack.

Shortly after starting my business I experienced the greatest adversity to date. My apartment had a new echo because all that was left was my desk, the bed, and my clothes hanging in the closet. The pressure of my entrepreneurship was too much for my wife. My family was gone.

The pain that followed lasted for months until the day my older daughter changed everything. "Hey Dad, I want to come live with you" she said in a very matter-of-fact, grown-up voice for an 8-year-old. I was having a hard time taking care of myself and the thought of being a single parent while running a brand new business seemed beyond my abilities. My logic and my fears were no match for her convincing argument of, "Dad I'll help you!" With that and her mother's approval I was not only running a business but I was also working at the most important role of my life – single dad.

I was determined to make it. I was determined to be a good example for my family and I was out to prove I wasn't just a guy who needed to buy a Sawzall. I could, and I would, be a successful young businessman in spite of my lack of experience. Just getting by was not an option. I had to make it big. I had to take some of the financial pressure off and be proud of what I accomplished. That was the beginning of working within my means but thinking outside of my limitations.

My first company, 1-800-Anytyme Home Services, didn't have the advantage of being first, second or even tenth in the Yellow Pages. In fact, it would have been easier for an ice cube to survive in a forest fire than for me to get my little company positioned in the first two-thirds of The Book. At that time your ads were positioned based on when you purchased your ad and the new guys had to take what was left. For many of us, that meant being near to last, seldom found, and never noticed.

Without being one of the first guys in the Yellow Pages I might as well have been invisible, I knew I had to find another way to get the phone to ring. That's when I turned to the Internet and became a student of internet marketing. Thankfully the Internet was the last thing on most service business owner's minds.

In spite of being a "closet" entrepreneur, I was able to get traction in my market and scoop up a good deal of customers using my new-found knowledge of internet marketing. Even with my initial success, I saw an inevitable obstacle on the horizon. The Internet was getting more and more popular and it was only a matter of time before my fierce competitors jumped on the bandwagon and tried to flush 1-800-Anytyme right out of the market.

I knew I had to find another way to get an edge on them.

# How I Survived the "Internet Gold Rush"

There's a saying in marketing: *"You don't have to be the best, only the first."*

While this is true, this philosophy also has an expiration date. When you succeed by "being first," people find out about it...people talk, people envy and eventually, people plot to backwards engineer your success.

This happened to a lot of people who caught the tidal wave of opportunity created by the rise in the popularity of the Internet. Some of those businesses are still around and doing even better today, but their present success has a lot to do with how they handled their past success.

One of their biggest secrets was they knew there was more to being the best than simply being first. A prime example is Yahoo. Yahoo was a great tool until Google came around. Likewise, when I was enjoying my early success as a closet Internet marketer, I knew it couldn't last forever.

As the Internet became more popular, I knew my competitors and I would be fighting over traffic. I knew there was not much I could do about it except to make sure I consistently converted that traffic into phone calls and sales. Otherwise, my competitors would use their bigger marketing budgets to bury me with larger and louder campaigns.

So there I was, at the top of my game. 1800Anytyme.com was dominating SEO rankings for all of San Diego County, Los Angeles County, Orange County, and Denver. I was also ruling Pay Per Click (PPC) in my local market with powerful PPC campaigns that were making my phone ring off the hook.

However, it did not take long before I noticed my website conversions slipping and my call count began its downward trend. I tried to improve both of them through trial and error, but I quickly realized I needed to consult some expert advice. I attended dozens of week-long Internet marketing seminars across the country, spending tens of thousands of dollars in my search for better answers. I was looking for that one expert that could help me master how to turn website visitors into actual service calls. It was an interesting experience and I learned a lot about what worked and most importantly, what didn't work. I knew there had to be some reason why visitors were landing on my site and bouncing off with rapid-fire speed.

The most important lesson I learned was that the best practice for getting traffic and converting sales had nothing to do with my marketing budget or even my business — It was all about the customer's level of trust. Seems obvious. People buy from people they trust. Nothing new there, right? Your ability to convert traffic into leads and sales will always boil down to how much trust your customer has in you.

But how do you get customers to trust you and believe you will add value?

Learning how to communicate trust to the customer came when I met Tim Ash, president of Site Turners and author of Landing Page Optimization. Tim stressed the importance of having credibility elements on my website and my mind took over from there.

I realized I needed to focus on generating positive feedback and began building online credibility through reviews on influential review sites. At first, I have to admit that the idea of hiring an offshore team to write reviews by the hundreds for just $2 an hour had momentarily crossed my mind. I was also approached by countless service providers who offered to use my real comment cards and then create fake accounts to write reviews by the hundreds.

I already knew too well the consequences of trying to fool God, I mean Google. I wasn't about to risk being banned from the most powerful search engine in the world and the source of nearly three-fourths of my business because I attempted to use questionable methods.

I decided against heading down the road of deceptive practices. My un-official mentors and business success icons, Tony Hsieh of Zappos and the late Steve Jobs of Apple, did not take short cuts. They created value not only for their customers but also their employees. They created companies people wanted to do business with and people who were proud to be their employees. That's exactly what I aspired to be.

That's when the unanswered questions started to whirl around in my head like a video game on steroids. How could I get my clients to talk positively about my service company? I could not manipulate them or the results. I knew the service I offered was reasonably priced and of high value, but those conclusions needed to come from my current customers and potential new customers needed to hear about it. I really wanted to properly leverage the many social platforms to build up my online reputation. I knew it was just a matter of learning how to do it the right way — with integrity.

Throughout the course of this book you will learn what took me countless hours of trial and error, not to mention loads of cash, to perfect. If there are any shortcuts to be taken, it's in learning from my mistakes and successes. I continue to observe, learn and completely immerse myself in the best, proven ways to create a remarkable company that has tremendous visibility and credibility. I have spent several years working with small, medium and large service companies on perfecting these strategies, which is why I knew the best way to support their success was to create an entire company to serve their needs. That passion led to launching ReviewBuzz.

I founded ReviewBuzz when I discovered an important link between top-notch customer service, online reviews and word-of-mouth marketing. ReviewBuzz.com is a comprehensive online system that helps service companies accumulate positive reviews and promote excellence in customer service. ReviewBuzz ties together measurement tools for automatically recognizing, tracking and gamifying the process of earning a positive review. The reward to the business owner is the organic way happy customers are motivated to post positive reviews, which allows the business to leverage those reviews to generate a power-selling buzz online.

Two years into its development, ReviewBuzz is helping thousands of companies generate reviews online which results in a significant increase in profitability. It gives me tremendous satisfaction to see the impact our efforts are making on service industries and I am proud that our team is completely committed to our motto: "Helping Good People Get Noticed."

But again, the intention of this book is to share proven strategies and help you grow your online reputation and your revenues by putting service first. This is also not solely a marketing strategies book, but an operational strategies resource. I am so excited about the successes that I've been able to create for our clients that I use their examples as a learning tool, not as a promotional stunt. I respect your investment of time to read this book and encourage you to find the applicable take-aways in the examples.

I am excited to know that when you finish this book you will be equipped with the same knowledge and

confidence that I have in knowing what it takes to Stop
Marketing. Be Remarkable!

# Chapter 1

# Your Most Valuable Marketing Asset Revealed

When you pick up a book that tells you to stop marketing, what goes through your mind? Does it make you a little nervous because it seems counterintuitive to everything you've heard in the past? Does it simply seem too good to be true? Will it negatively affect your profits?

It's not too good to be true, it's not the complete opposite of good business practices, and it *will* improve your bottom line. The best part is you are guaranteed to see your work environment become more exciting than ever. The tools I will present to you are not merely a twist on traditional marketing techniques. In fact, they leave traditional marketing in the dust, where it belongs and instead they focus on what creates exceptional companies.

Many organizations do very little actual marketing when their business is booming, and yet frantically start marketing again when times are leaner. Sound familiar? Don't be embarrassed, we have all been there at one time or another. Marketers and Small to Medium-sized Business (SMB) owners and admittedly myself put all of the emphasis and a 100 percent of our marketing budget on lead generation and self-promoting content. That was when getting the phone to ring was done by solely smart marketing and that meant business was good and we could take a sigh of relief that bills were getting paid. But times have changed and rather than try to hold steadfast to old techniques and wait out what you believe is a short-lived trend, it's time to be proactive.

# Prioritizing Post Sale Engagement

For the last decade online marketing strategies have always been centered around lead generation. How do we optimize our web properties to perform better and drive more leads? Getting more traffic building a better mousetrap to capture more leads has been the hot topic and continues to be for all of us marketers.

In the service industry leads are everything and lead generation was my primary responsibility. I became skilled at building out my company's web properties and PPC campaigns so I ranked higher and performed better than even our biggest competitors.

I have always gravitated towards being the chief architect around improving lead generation and outsmarting our competition by simply focusing on the latest and greatest marketing techniques. Until one day I realized that this lead generation thing started taking on a very interesting shift. I am a strong believer in looking at the most advanced and competitive markets outside of my industry and keeping an eye out for signals for the next big shift in marketing. Being successful is not always about being the inventor. There is much to be gained from not reinventing the wheel, but rather watching trends and innovators and applying those lessons in a new and creative way to your own circumstances.

My breakthrough came when I found that Amazon consumers were starting to weigh in on products and were influencing prospective shoppers. I looked at the comments, ratings and quantity of reviews to ultimately determine what to buy. Amazon was a pioneer of using customer feedback to help consumers make better choices. Better choices meant happy and repeat buyers.

The reason this book is in your hands is because you realize the rules have changed. No longer is it only about lead generation. Now it's crucial that SMB's pay close attention to Post Sale engagement and stop focusing solely on marketing. Post Sale is all about being remarkable. First, be remarkable and then, market. Otherwise you are putting the cart before the horse.

Keeping your customers engaged after the sale is not just a good business practice, it will also determine whether your business thrives or dies a slow but certain death.

Post Sale is the level of engagement your business and employees have created through your customer service experience. Will they recommend you? Will they like you on Facebook or +1 you on Google's social network G+? Are they more likely to become your biggest fan or a Ranter who will become a detractor of future business? These are the questions you need to ask yourself after every transaction.

If you continue to travel the path without understanding the importance of Post Sale you will end up with what I call the broken bucket syndrome.

# The Broken Bucket Syndrome

Imagine you are effortlessly floating downriver and without notice your boat rapidly starts taking on water, and you are heading towards the rapids. You look for help and the first tool you think of is that old, trusty bucket to bail out the water. Only the bucket is no longer trusty, in fact it doesn't work the way it used to — it's filled with holes. Not only is it ineffective, it impedes your ability to look for more effective tools. You know it's worked in the past so you are committed to sticking with it. Instead of being more alert to finding other possibilities, you try desperately to fix the bucket — you use valuable resources to fill the holes to no avail. All of this extra effort is costing you precious time and money.

That's exactly what happens when you continue to neglect the importance of Post Sale Engagement. What you didn't realize is the holes that have emerged in the old way of doing things are in the form of a poor or even nonexistent online reputation, jeopardizing your credibility. It's time to throw out the bucket and open your eyes. There are new, better, more reliable methods to stay afloat and enjoy the strong currents of a growing, profitable business.

The tools I will show you are more than pieces of duct tape for your old bucket, they are water-proof ways to show potential new customers they can trust you enough to hire you without reservation. Would that make your marketing efforts easier? Would that help reduce the extreme fluctuation in your revenues? You bet it will.

When I say stop marketing, be remarkable, I am referring to the need for changing our thinking by being exceptional and not just relying on fancy self-promoting marketing campaigns. Embrace today's tools that will supercharge your marketing campaigns by creating a recipe that includes your customers. Today's consumers don't trust old-school marketing as a stand-alone source for purchase decisions. In fact, only 23 percent of consumers trust the self-promoted company content they read online, such as your websites, blogs, and advertisements. (Source: *Trust Agents: Using the Web to Build Influence, Improve Reputation, and Earn Trust*, Chris Brogan and Julien Smith, Wiley Press, 2010)

So what's the answer to achieving both higher profits and growth by simply focusing on what you do best? It's simpler than you might think and I am looking forward to sharing all that I have learned through countless hours and thousands of dollars' worth of advice and research.

I will be introducing you to what could be the *single most remarkable* marketing secret you'll learn about online marketing so far. Don't put off learning and implementing the tools you will acquire here because it is just a matter of time (a very short time) until your competition will become a master at using these strategies and you'll be struggling just to catch up.

Let's start with a key concept.

# Optimizing the Impact of Positive UGC

Oh, I know what you're thinking... *"Not another acronym."* What is UGC? Ever seen those comic books where the characters' words appear in little conversation bubbles above their heads? Now imagine those characters are consumers. What if someone copied those little conversations and pasted them all over a big billboard for everyone to see? That's UGC.

I know, it might sound a little far-fetched, but what I just described is happening right now on the Internet. Conversations between consumers are taking place in cyberspace, and the words aren't disappearing once they're spoken. Instead, the users of the Internet are creating their own content, and that's UGC.

UGC is "User Generated Content."

What's so remarkable about UGC? Ever heard of word-of-mouth marketing? Of course you have. UGC is simply word-of-mouth marketing gone digital.

Consider this: A customer is searching for your service online. They find you and your competitor's listings side by side on Google. Your listing has dozens and dozens of quality customer reviews and impeccable rating scores and your competitor has a few low ratings with mixed and infrequent reviews.

**Examples of UGC:**
- *Comments on blogs or review sites (like Google+, Yahoo Local, Yelp, YellowPages.com, City Search, Local.com, Angie's List etc.)*
- *Posts on Facebook*
- *Tweets*
- *Blogs written by consumers*
- *Posts on forums or forum threads*
- *Any content about your company that is created by someone outside of your company*

Can you finish this story without my help? Of course you can. It's a UGC TKO baby!

Those outstanding, highly-rated reviews are a powerful form of UGC, and you're about to discover how leveraging User Generated Content can help you rule your competition, explode your sales power and build a company culture that will make your employees so excited about their job, they may not want to go home.

Can you see how what a customer says about you will always outweigh the greatest sales copy, the slickest web design and provide better *service* than your competitor? The good news is online reviews can validate your company, but you need to get your customers to tell that story.

In a desperate attempt to get your potential customers' attention you can burn up thousands of dollars a week calling in expert marketing consultants, direct response copywriters, PPC and Search Engine Optimization (SEO) geeks, and masters of branding and design. However, if your competition has the power of positive UGC in their corner and you don't, they'll bury you right next to Jimmy Hoffa.

This is reality, and it's not changing any time soon. People judge the value of companies, products and services based on what their peers and even complete strangers are saying on the Internet. Wouldn't you?

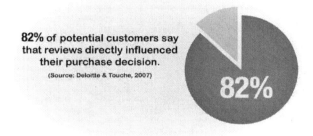

82% of potential customers say that reviews directly influenced their purchase decision. (Source: Deloitte & Touche, 2007)

82%

Today's consumers are the most well-educated customers in history. Thanks to the Internet, information is now at their fingertips, showing them everything they want to know about you and your competitors.

A review is a review right? Wrong. The value of a review is very different and it comes down to one thing — traffic. Just like in real estate, having the right location for your reviews is a critical element of success.

The key question is…

# Are You Putting the Power of Reviews (UGC) to Work for YOU?

Putting UGC to work isn't just about gathering reviews and posting them online. Let's consider the location element of real estate for a minute. You know the three key principles to successful real estate investing right? Location, location, location. If I put up a 12-bedroom mansion with an indoor heated pool, two tennis courts, and a rose garden in a neighborhood where there are bars on every window, I'd have a hard time selling it for a fraction of what I'd invested in it, right?

The same concept applies to reviews.

A great review posted on a highly-respected review site holds far more value than one listed on a site with no brand recognition, traffic or any social influence. A review on a site that lacks brand recognition will not produce many, if any, clicks or calls. It's like the difference between having an ad for your company on a billboard in Times Square versus posting a sign in the restroom of a bar that serves fifty-cent drafts from 10 to 11 p.m. It's all about location. You want your reviews posted on popular and highly influential review sites with traffic and a loyal user community.

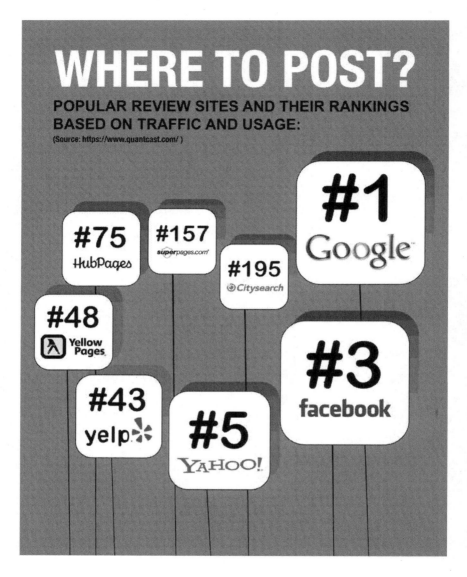

**WHERE TO POST?**
POPULAR REVIEW SITES AND THEIR RANKINGS
BASED ON TRAFFIC AND USAGE:
(Source: https://www.quantcast.com/ )

#75 HubPages
#157 superpages.com
#195 Citysearch
#1 Google
#48 Yellow Pages
#43 yelp
#5 YAHOO!
#3 facebook

The Internet is like a great big virtual Monopoly board and your objective is to have your company reviews on the side of Park Place and Boardwalk, where your customers will not only land, but are (1) highly influential, (2) trustworthy and (3) highly trafficked.

When a review site has these three things working for it, you can bet consumers will trust what's written on the site.

## Visibility Does Not Equal Credibility

Chances are you've heard this one before...

"It's not what you know that matters, it's who you know."

Sounds great, right? If only it was that easy. In the book *Social Media Boom,* Jeffery Gitomer explains that it's not who you know, it's who knows you. Okay, now we're getting closer to reality. But we're still not zeroed in on the great secret of marketing success.

You probably already have dozens or even hundreds of people who know about your business. They've driven by your building or they've seen you online. Maybe you have a few commercials on TV or you've created some YouTube videos. Maybe a lot of them have already done business with you. They know who you are, that's for sure.

But here's the one thing that makes all the difference, "What are your customers *saying* about you?"

Many businesses only think about this when a customer has a complaint. That's when they become a whirlwind of motivation. They'll do whatever it takes to make the customer happy or, at the very least, get them to remove a bad review. They'll give away free stuff, apologize profusely, and call them "Sir" or "Ma'am" 72 times per minute and endlessly bend over backwards.

The bottom line is that too many business owners are only aware of their customers' opinions when it has negative consequences. Beyond that, they assume "quiet customers must be happy customers." Okay, maybe it's true. Maybe your customers are completely ecstatic about you. Maybe they have a picture of you and your company logo right next to the picture of their family pet. However, if they're not talking about how great you are, and if they're not posting glowing reviews online where your potential customers can see them, it doesn't mean squat.

Here's what you *should* be worried about...

## Are You Circling the Drain with Misbelief?

When social media first started, I was like many other SMB's; I thought it was something to be used only for personal sharing and by other people. But it didn't take long to see what was happening. Visibility from these types of online sites was gaining momentum and the tide was shifting. This was not a fad and other companies were leveraging it to build their business not just hold onto what they had.

If you figured you'd wait it out and stick to what you know best, you are losing money every day. You are holding on to the notion that when the economy bounces back everything will be okay. You are hanging on to the edge and it won't take long before you get swept away.

Like it or not, this is not a fad. This is also not sometime in the distant future. It's happening now and rather than sit back and wait for what you believe will fade away, you need to take action. You can't afford to ride it out and here's why.

Imagine this, you log onto your bank account online. The balance is $100,000.00 (Sounds nice eh?), but after looking at the balance for about five seconds you notice it drops to $99,995.00.

What the &@#$!?
After 10 seconds...
$99,985.000

...15 seconds...
$99,970.00

...20...
$99,950.00

...25...
$99, 925.00

...30...
$99,895.00

Wow, someone turn off the faucet before your entire business circles the drain.

How fast would you be on the phone with your bank? I'm guessing pretty darn fast. Yet as you're reading this, the same thing is happening to your business capital. It's slipping away from you like cell phone minutes on a teenager's calling plan...and it's likely you don't even know it.

How is this possible?

You have your balance sheet where you track income and expenses and monitor your profit margins. You have an Obsessive Compulsive super nerd of an accountant on your payroll and a CPA who's so slick he's got tax loopholes named after him.

But you're not getting the whole story.

Your balance sheet isn't helping you zero in on the parasites that are eating away at your most valuable asset — the asset which, if lost or damaged, could easily put you out of business. That asset is your *online reputation,* and the operative word here is "online." Remember that the online world is not only accessible to anyone, anywhere in the world it's also written in something more permanent than ink. When someone writes a review about your company on a highly influential and highly trafficked review site, it stays there. It's probably the most permanent medium in history for recording human thoughts and ideas and making sure they don't get erased. Think about that in relation to building your company reputation and becoming socially trusted.

So how do you protect your reputation with the advent of online reviews and other forms of UGC? By capitalizing on and optimizing what many experts refer to as Social Proof.

Social Proof is your business' ability to be trusted and endorsed by others, by people who are "speaking to" your potential customers online on highly influential social recommendation sites such as Yahoo Local, Facebook, and Google+. These recommendations are referred to as social signals and when they are positive it indicates you are socially trusted, therefore giving you social proof and also increasing your search engine results.

Picture Social Proof as a collection of popularity votes with big stacks of dollar bills attached to them.

Social Proof tells people your company has earned the trust of previous customers by getting the job done well.

This can translate to dollar signs so big that one "popularity vote" not only equals hundreds or even thousands of real dollar bills, but it can reproduce dollar bills over and over again. Building Social Proof is the closest thing to printing money there is (unless you happen to be Ben Bernanke).

There's also a big difference between capital and capital production capability. I know, it sounds complicated. But in his book *The Seven Habits of Highly Effective People*, the late Stephen Covey explained the concept of capital production capability simply with Aesop's fable about the Goose and the golden eggs.

As a refresher, the story goes…a farmer has a goose that lays one golden egg every day. That would seem like a great asset to have, right? But rather than foster and care for the goose the farmer gets greedy and decides to kill the goose, cut it open and get ALL the eggs out in one shot.

What's the result? Of course he ends up with a great big proverbial goose egg. Zero. Nada. Zilch.

Before you judge the farmer too quickly, realize that you (and I) have done the exact same thing. We've been so focused on producing those golden eggs that we neglected the very thing which can help us produce them over and over again – providing remark-*able* service. Most companies do this. They have balance sheets where they keep track of their earnings. They apply a simple equation that looks something like this…Dollars In > Dollars Out = Don't Worry, Be Happy ☺

Okay, so we've got a steady flow of dollars coming in and we're making more than we're spending. Works for me… but here's the million-dollar question: Who's Taking Care of the Goose?

If you had a balance sheet to track your social proof and your capital production capacity, what would it look like? If you're not sure, you're probably in the red. I know, I know. If your customers aren't complaining then you're doing well, right? In essence, the goose must still be alive. Yes, but the goose might also be malnourished and emaciated. Meanwhile, your competitors could be taking great care of their goose. They are feeding it well, putting it up in a nest threaded from cashmere and with a first-class P90x coach training it to bench press Buicks and compete in Olympic level games of Duck, Duck, Goose.

Right now, your competition might already be making strides towards learning to gain massive social signals and positive reviews with high ratings and putting them right in front of hundreds or even thousands of *your* would-be customers. Guess what's happening with every positive review being posted by your competitors while your customers admire your wonderful services in modest silence?

$99,985.000
...15 seconds...

$99,970.00
...20 seconds...

$99,950.00
...25 seconds...

This is happening right now. Someone somewhere is amassing hundreds and hundreds of real reviews, and they're using them to collect more customers, provide more great service and solicit more positive reviews.

The clock is ticking...

I think the answer is clear: If you're not managing your online reputation with the best tools available, you're losing money.

If nothing changes, it will essentially keep costing you new (and repeat) business until you make a shift. Bottom line, without trust signals your Social Proof is leaking out and you need to plug the hole and rebuild the flow NOW!

Your capital production capability is *directly related to your social proof,* and whether you like it or not, that reputation is based ninety-nine percent on what online information is available about your company. These days, your potential customer isn't interested in making judgments based solely on what they see on their computer, TV, or even on a billboard the size of their house. Contrary to what we've believed for years, your company website is not your primary marketing tool on the Internet, it's not even close.

After all, why should a consumer take your word for it when they can simply whip out their laptop or mobile device, type your name or the name of your service into a search bar and do their information gathering on their own terms?

Therefore, if you're not managing and proactively leveraging your online reputation, you're losing money, guaranteed. You're gambling with your most valuable asset by hoping your positive reviews will simply grow by themselves. They won't, and those who know this and who heed my advice will dominate their market and squash their competition like a grape.

The great news is that if you have a good reputation online, it's easy to get new business. So what makes for a good reputation online? It starts with your employees. Is the first contact a customer has with your company impressive? Are they extremely happy with the service you provided? Not just satisfied, but happy? Is the post-sale contact from your company respectful and courteous?

Now let's finish the cycle of how having a good reputation makes getting new business easy. The logic that follows is when it's easy to get new business; it's easy to keep your employees happy and productive. When your employees are happy and productive, it's easy to keep your customers happy and saying great things about you. When your customers are saying great things about you on a consistent basis and you know how to turn that feedback into positive online reviews, your goose gets bigger and healthier and starts laying more golden eggs. Add all this up and you've got the closest thing to a monopoly as legally possible.

Now, here's why you need this book to make that happen...

"What others say about you and your product, service, or business is at least 1000% more convincing than what you say, even if you are 1000% more eloquent"

Dan Kennedy
Multi-millionaire entrepreneur, trusted marketing advisor, consultant and coach

# The Five Rules of Being Remarkable

For businesses and even expert marketers, getting authentic positive customer reviews can be harder than getting new customers. True, the best salesperson might be a happy customer, but only if you know how to hire them to start selling for you. It's not enough to just give good service anymore; you must know how to sell your customers on *why they should sell you.*

The great merchant entrepreneur James Cash Penny (founder of J.C Penny) once said,

*"A merchant who approaches business with the idea of serving the public well has nothing to fear from the competition." - James Cash Penny*

Amen to that Mr. J.C.P. There was a time when that was true, but now it needs an amendment...

*"The merchant who approaches business with the idea of serving the public well **and getting the public to talk about them** has nothing to fear from the competition."*

BAM!!!

Sorry, I got a little excited there. But that's because I know how powerful this can be once you get it working for you. Just as with the acquisition of new customers, there's a reasonably predictable and "duplicatable" system you can use to get dozens or even hundreds of customer reviews every month and turn your shy and quiet customer base into an army of jabber-jawed sales superstars... and you don't even have to put them on your payroll.

Great! Here's the plan...

This book contains five essential rules you can use to get reviews working for you right away, and without spending *any* extra money on marketing:

1.   Don't "We-We" All Over Yourself

2.   Power Your Profits through Remark-ability

3.   Turn Reviews into Revenue

4.   Beware the "Fool's Gold" of Internet Marketing

5.   Build a Buzz-Winning Team

Let's get started...

# Chapter One Summary

1. User Generated Content (UGC) is word-of-mouth marketing gone digital.

2. It's not who you know, but who knows you that's important to marketing and growing your business.

3. If you can get enough people saying positive things about your business in the right place or using the right social recommendation sites, you will have a steady stream of new and repeat customers who will consistently grow your business.

4. Social Proof refers to your business' ability to be trusted and endorsed by others, by people who are *speaking to* your potential customers online.

5. Your capital production capability is *directly related to your social proof,* and whether you like it or not, that reputation is based ninety-nine percent on what online information is available about your business.

# Chapter One Recommended Reading

*Crush It!: Why NOW Is the Time to Cash In on Your Passion,*
Gary Vaynerchuk (Harper Studio, 2009)

*Winning the Zero Moment of Truth – ZMOT,* Jim Lecinski
(Vook, 2011)

For convenience,
a list of ZMOT resources provided
by Google can be found at:
**SMBRbook.com/zmot**

# Chapter 2:

# Rule 1: Don't "We-We" All Over Yourself

To become remarkable, you need to look at marketing in a whole new light and play by a different set of rules. You've been programed for the last few years to think one way — that when it comes to marketing it's you against the world.

In the past, the name of the game was to shout louder than your competitors. The rules were simple: Get into the Yellow Pages early for the best placement, grind and negotiate with the sales rep, then list your "benefits" and "unique selling proposition" in your ads and create an appealing brand personality. Spend time tracking the results and see if you're getting a return on your investment then repeat the same process for as many directory books as possible.

Marketing was once all about singing your own praises as loudly as possible and in all the right places. Today, it's no longer simply a matter of your company broadcasting its self-promoting message to the world. Now that same self-promotion can hurt your business.

## Are You "We-We-ing" All Over Yourself?

These days, you can jump up on the highest stump in the land and shout out all you want about yourself but you'll only end up like the proverbial tree that fell in the forest... No one hears it, no one comes to see what happened, and nothing is left but a rotting stump.

You can try shouting louder, longer and more often saying things like:

*"We have the fastest service in town!"*

*"We have the best trained employees!"*

*"We have 24-hour service!"*

*"We will beat any competitor's price!"*

*"We love our customers!"*

*"We have 30 years of experience!"*

"We, we we..." all the way home.

In the new age of social media, you can "we-we" until you're drowning in it, but all it takes is a few keystrokes for a potential customer to find out what *the rest of the world* thinks about you!

**TARGETED TIPS**

Today, it's no longer important what you say about yourself. It's what your customers are saying that counts.

"We-We Marketing" results are slowing, and in the near future, it won't make a bit of difference as a stand-alone marketing plan. To achieve the desired results, you must learn to blend the traditional marketing of the past with the newly emerging UGC marketing (remember User Generated Content). You can continue to we-we everyone and you might fool a few, but if you can't back it up with great service, anyone smart enough to Google you will end up pulling back the curtain and revealing the truth.

Decades of being assaulted by marketing messages have left consumers deeply despising being sold to. Today, because of modern online tools, such as review sites, they can find out the truth about your company within seconds of seeing your ad.

To illustrate this point, and to prove that it's *already created astounding results,* let's take a look at one of the biggest triumphs of word-of-mouth marketing over we-we marketing....

## How Pepsi Challenged the King of Pop (Not Michael Jackson)

Back in the 1980s Pepsi became one of the first companies to ask for their customers' help in giving Coca Cola, one of the world's most powerful brands, a run for its money. As you know, Coca Cola has such a powerful brand that many people refer to any dark soda pop as "Coke." Someone at Pepsi was confident that in spite of Coke's image power, Pepsi was still the better tasting product.

Most companies would have chosen to create a clever marketing campaign making claims like this...

We taste better than Coke!
We have a sweeter flavor!
We have a smoother finish and aftertaste!

We, we, we...and probably a lot of wasted marketing dollars.

But Pepsi was confident that if they could get unbiased consumer opinions on their side, Coke would only be left to fight back using "we-we" marketing.

That led to "The Pepsi Challenge."

This is a prime example of how one company, well before its time, stood up to we-we marketing and started harnessing the power of consumer opinion to prove the value of its product.

Blind taste tests were given to thousands of consumers who tasted a sample of Coke and a sample of Pepsi. This stripped Coke of its image power and let the consumer make a decision based on taste alone. The tests were done at malls and shopping

For convenience, a list of case studies such as Pepsi and Apple can be found at: SMBRbook.com/case-studies

centers with regular consumers, not people who had been paid to pick Pepsi over Coke and the results were recorded with hidden video cameras. It didn't take long before television commercials were streaming these blind taste test videos over and over again. This real-life, "live" reviews were undeniable.

Just think about the power of the message here. One company is saying *"We're the best,"* and the other company has thousands of consumers behind them saying *"No, they're the best."* The results completely vindicated Pepsi and actually scared Coke into altering their formula, something which turned out to be a huge mistake for the "King of Pop."

## The Rise of the Internet and the Overthrow of Monopoly Advertising

In the late 20th century the Internet came to put an end to the reign of Ole Yeller. The Yellow Pages was the ultimate pay-or-be-invisible concept of marketing. But the early days of the Internet had its own type of monopoly advertising.

In the beginning there was no World Wide Web — it was just a bunch of geeks with slow dial-up modems hosting bulletin boards. Then along came CompuServe and AOL. These two giants controlled all the content you saw while on their "sites." Once again, if you wanted to be listed you had to pay the man.

Then the Worldwide Web erupted, allowing people to create their own websites. This was the beginning of the "Wild West" days of the Internet. Only instead of the fastest gun winning it was all about being the first on the scene.

You got yourself a covered wagon (web hosting), and went out and claimed your territory (your domain name) and started digging your gold mine. The problem was no one knew how to find you. You still had to advertise your website in your Yellow Page ads and on your brochures and business cards.

Then along came online directories. Someone came up with the brilliant idea of making the equivalent of the Yellow Pages online by listing websites. Nothing really changed except the medium. It was still essentially We-We Marketing and quick-draw showdowns.

Next came search engines. Search engines didn't charge any money to list your website! They were a liberating force for service companies, leveling the playing field and freeing business owners from the bondage of Yellow Page advertising.

The Calvary had arrived!

There was only one problem, in order to show up in the search engines you needed the right content on your website. You needed certain keywords, meta tags and domain names. From this, Search Engine Optimization (SEO) was born.

Those who caught on to SEO and landed on Page One of Google and the other main search engines got all the calls. It turned out to be not quite as liberating as we had hoped. Now you had to hire an SEO expert in place of paying for Yellow Pages ads — or *in addition* to paying for Yellow Page ads!

But SEO was easy in those days. All you needed was to mention the keyword for your site three or four times every one hundred words and your site got a high ranking. You might remember the sites that looked like this:

*"We-We" Chiropractic Services*

*If you need chiropractic services, we've got chiropractic services here. Come get your chiropractic services because we have the best chiropractic services in town. We have chiropractic services!*

But of course, as the technology of the Internet became more advanced things became more complex. There was link building, multiple directory listings, PPC, landing pages, viral marketing, email marketing, and on and on. It seemed like there was some new daily trick you had to learn if you wanted to stay ahead of the competition.

Then something happened that changed everything...

# The Arrival of Web 2.0: How the West Was Won

As the 21st Century got into full swing Web 2.0 was born — the *interactive* web. The Internet became more about *people* communicating with *people* — many to many — rather than just one to many. It seemed to happen overnight.

Anyone with access to a computer could broadcast their voice and opinions online. Consumers could create their own web pages on MySpace. They could start their own groups and forums on sites such as Yahoo. They could have their own blogs on sites like Blogger.com. It wasn't long before they could share their experiences and rate service companies on Yelp and Google Local.

*That's how the online review was born and how the once Wild West of the Internet was won.*

Today, consumers are no longer deaf, dumb, and blind. They don't simply throw darts to choose a service company. They no longer have to listen while marketers talk. Today, they can see, hear and talk to each other about what's going on at your company as well as with your competition.

*With Web 2.0 customers went from having no power to now having the power to do more good or bad for your company that you could ever do yourself, no matter how much you spend on Yellow Page ads, direct marketing, SEO, blogging, PPC ads and so on.*

Here's the point of this little history lesson: Your customers went from having *no power* to having the power to *do more good or bad marketing for your company than you could ever do for yourself.* It doesn't matter how much you spend on Yellow Page ads, direct marketing, SEO, blogging, PPC ads and so on, you'll never have as much influence on the buying decision as the voices of your customers.

## Are You Ready to Catch the Wave of Online Word-of-Mouth Marketing?

For the past 20 years, online service marketing has been evolving so fast it's impossible for one person to keep up just by understanding the latest technologies and trends. The good news is that if you understand how the evolution of online technology has impacted buying behaviors, you won't have to spin your wheels chasing trends.

You'll be able to predict and create trends.

While you're spending your time reading blogs and attending seminars on the latest Internet marketing strategies and tactics, a team of top-shelf geeks has been in the back room at Google playing double agent. They're thinking up new ways to give consumers the edge and then figuring out how to make more money helping companies like yours reach those consumers. They have a *huge* workforce and billions of dollars to spend.

TARGETED **TIPS**

*TRUST is the new trend in search.*

They also have new programs coming out on a consistent basis which they're using to create more trust with the public. In 2012 they launched the Google Trusted Stores program.

This program allows online "stores" to have their customer service practices monitored by Google for a 28-day period. If at the end of the four weeks Google feels the store has performed up to Google Trusted Store standards, they become an official Google Trusted Store.

Can you guess what Google measures to determine whether or not a store is worthy of being labeled as "trusted?" Check out the guidelines as stated by Google:

## Qualifications to Become A Google "Trusted Store"
- US Merchants only, English as the primary language on the website
- Clearly Visible Terms of Service, Privacy Policy, Returns, and Shipping policies
- No selling of Google Prohibited Items.
- Drop shippers are allowed, but not through ready-made drop shipping sites.
- Merchants must charge the card and cause an item to be shipped.
- Accurate inventory availability at all times

## Performance Requirements
- On-time shipping of more than 90%
- More than 100 orders on a rolling 28 day basis
- More than 50% trackable shipments
- 90% of orders must have an actual ship date within 3 days of estimated ship date
- Average time to shipments less than or equal to 14 days
- Less than 2.5% cancellation rate
- Less than 10% of orders are pre-orders or backorders
- Merchant must respond to the customer questions within 2 business days 99% of the time
- 99% resolution rate to customer questions within 2 business days
- 100% of refunds within 2 days if product does not have to be returned by customers (or within 6 days of receipt of a returned item).
- Google code on every page to track shoppers, and code to pass data back to Google on the receipt/thank-you page.
- Code, Manual entry, or a data feed to pass tracking numbers, cancellations, and refunds back to Google for measurement.

## Steps to Become Member of Google Trusted Stores
1. Place the Google Trusted Stores code on your website
2. Google monitors your shipping and customer service for 28 days
3. If your store meets the Trusted Store requirements, your site becomes a Google Trusted Store

Are you starting to see the trend here? It's about trust, and the more programs Google rolls out, the more important trust will become in the online marketplace. It doesn't stop with Google either. As you know, Bing has teamed up with Facebook to bring a social dimension to their search experience also.

The entire online search experience is going social. Don't you think it would be a good idea for search engine *marketing* to follow? This is the trend that you need to catch, and if you do you could end up becoming one of the companies that everyone in your industry is talking about.

Companies with websites were the ones reaping the rewards when directories came around. Those who understood SEO and started optimizing their sites after search engines came online dominated with top rankings. The companies that caught the wave of Pay Per Click advertising got tons of great leads for pennies a click. Many companies jumped on multiple forms of media becoming important to search engines and they began adding blogs and videos to their web presence. They caught the wave right on its crest.

That is exactly what I want to do for you — give you a head start on your competition. Most likely, your competitors don't know the secrets being revealed in this book. This is your chance to *get it* before they do so you can ride the new wave to the top.

*Notice that as each new technology
came online it was the companies
who caught the next new wave
that dominated their online market.*

## Online Word-of-Mouth Marketing Is the New Sheriff in Town

The Internet has changed the way people make buying decisions, *both offline and online.*

Today's consumers don't have to sit at their TV or their radio listening to advertisements. They have TIVO, iTunes, Netflix, XM Radio, spam filters, caller ID, pop-up blockers and dozens of other gadgets which are designed to do one thing — *rid their lives of interruptive marketing.*

For decades, people have put up with the interruption of advertisements, even in the early days of the Internet when the web had no interactive features. But what did consumers do the moment they had the option to control whether or not they had to view or listen to advertisements? They turned the ads off. They tuned them out. In an attempt not to lose the consumer's attention, television providers responded by increasing the volume of commercials higher than the regular programming. The public complained and the Federal Communications Commission (FCC) passed rules to regulate the volume. Effective December 13, 2012 all broadcast providers had to adjust the volume of advertisements to match their programming. This is a great example of how the public is forcing changes simply by having more avenues in which to be heard.

Just as the public uses the Internet to voice their opinions they also use it to gather information on their *own terms* and they are not looking for advertisements. They now have direct access to hundreds of thousands of reviews written by other consumers, and that's exactly what they're looking for — social proof.

If you only get one point out of this chapter, make it this: Social media, in all its forms, is the perfect place for word-of-mouth marketing to flourish. That's it.

Today the average Facebook user has roughly 200 friends. When one of them recommends your company, that recommendation is available for all of those friends to see. What that means is with every Facebook recommendation you receive, you've laid out no additional money to reach potentially hundreds of new customers. Your customer is essentially telling all their friends that they are happy to have done business with you and suggesting that their friends might be just as happy with your services.

By "liking" your company they are supporting you, simply clicking on "like" shows up on their recent activities. By giving you a high rating or score and a raving review on a trusted and influential review site, your customers are saying to anyone who views it they think your company provides value and that you're trustworthy. That's digital word-of-mouth marketing at its most powerful.

The big, fat, cash-gobbling mistake most service companies make is treating social media marketing like direct marketing. They shovel out tons of money to web designers to have fancy looking Facebook pages and Twitter pages created just so they can say, "Oh yeah, we're doing social media marketing. We've got a Facebook page and we post on it once a day and we have over 300 likes most of which are prospects that are not even within our service area. We've got Twitter and YouTube and..."

But that's not what it's about.

Social media marketing is, by definition, social. If you're just posting advertisements or links to your sites and blurbs about your company on your Facebook, Twitter and in your YouTube videos, you're not really doing social media marketing — you are doing we-we marketing on social media platforms.

## The Difference Between We-We Marketing and Social Media Marketing

Look at most companies' Facebook pages and Twitter accounts and they'll read like a billboard or a Yellow Page ad — they are pushy and obnoxious, and leave you feeling more like they're talking *at* you rather than talking *to* you. "We, we, we, we, we..." they say.

TARGETED TIPS

*Today, social rank is more important than search rank.*

The true goal of social media marketing is to create an environment that is conducive to generating and multiplying social buzz between your customers as well as to create a link from your existing customers to your prospective customers. This is a much different process than the traditional forms of marketing like advertising, websites, SEO, Yellow Page advertising, direct mailing, email marketing, and TV/Radio ads which are becoming less and less effective these days.

Sure, you can create a long list of impressive videos, dazzling websites, and custom keyword-tailored landing pages. But if you really want to get some buzz going and dominate your market, then increase your social footprint and begin building an online community that will translate into social capital, then get into conversations with your customers. Ten years ago, the Internet had not progressed much farther than simply being an electronic Yellow Pages directory as far as businesses were concerned. When you searched for a dentist, you got a list of dentists, nothing else. No additional help. Since then the web has become a social animal that has changed dramatically, it's a whole new ball game for businesses wanting to take advantage of the Internet's incredible power and reach.

Surely you know about Facebook's $104 billion IPO evaluation. Why is Facebook so valuable in the online marketplace? Because they're creating value for people by meeting the basic human need for connection and significance. Facebook gives people a chance to publicly voice their opinions and to stay connected with people who they haven't caught up with since high school. Thanks to Facebook, you never have to worry about losing touch with someone because you lost their address, phone number or email. If you're connected through Facebook, you're connected for life.

Because of this, Facebook is threatening to become more relevant than Google and Google knows it! That's why Google started their own social network, Google+, and integrated it into their search results. Now, if you are signed into Google+ and you do a search on Google, you not only see their business-as-usual search results, but you see entries that have been given a "+1" on Google+, as well as links to companies, brands, and places that your circle of friends have recommended and reviewed.

Google isn't the only company that realizes what's happening. Dozens of review sites like Yelp, Zagat and Angie's List are becoming more popular because they're in the business of offering trust to consumers through the sharing of real customer reviews. All these online giants are realizing that no one can sell a company brand like the *customer can sell the brand.* These days, smart brands are doing more than taking advantage of social networks. They're allowing their customers to become co-creators on their company brand. That's powerful stuff, my friends.

## One Size Doesn't Fit All

*customers* are working hand in hand with *companies* to create today's most trusted brands

Have you ever been to a social media marketing seminar or read articles about how to use Facebook to grow your business? What have you noticed about many of these sources of marketing information? The tactics don't always apply to certain service industries. Sure, they will tell you the strategies are universal and to be proactive about getting your buy-in they tell you about that rare exception when a plumber, electrician or heating company increased their incoming calls by fifty percent over a 60-day period because one piece of content went viral. But these numbers are not sustainable and those results are far from the norm.

Customers aren't looking to learn about what their plumber has to say and they don't want to be "besties" with their roofer. That's never what social media has been about. It works for organic food stores and cool things like music bands where you want to know the latest and greatest updates. But when it comes to service businesses, c'mon lets be real. When someone is in need of service for the most part it's a decision they don't plan months or weeks ahead and your occasional Facebook post is going to have no impact on you driving a customer to your business.

One size does not fit all. Instead, there is more to engaging online than Facebook and Twitter. Don't get me wrong, I believe you should have a presence on these popular networks when your customer is trying to find you, but don't sink too much of your time and resources into pushing out content when you are certain to be 10 times more successful earning social proof by providing remark-*able* service. Your time and resources are better spent on creating an exceptional customer experience.

So instead of looking for "friends" and hoping to get retweeted, let's concentrate on earning social trust. Besides, the day is fast approaching when "people rank" will replace the way search engines currently rank website pages. While keywords and incoming links still have the power to increase your search results, they can be a result of manipulation. Because of this many consumers are skeptical and they are giving more weight to what others are saying about you. Consider how difficult it will be for less ethical companies to manipulate the system when page rank is determined by public consensus? They won't be able to unless they step up their game with exceptional service or products and become the preferred company. What you can do is get a head start on them and inspire your customers to talk about you online. If you wait until people rank defeats keywords and incoming links and is crowned the new ruler of search, your competition will catch on first and own your market. Don't worry; I will get into great detail about how to inspire your customers to talk about you in the upcoming chapters.

If you want to create a raving fan club (your social capital) and you want to make your competition green with envy, you have to understand the principles of socially driven marketing. I know it sounds intimidating and seems like a lot of work but we're not talking about a virtual cult where your company logo is tattooed on every one of your customers. What's important to remember is you are trying to engage your customers and encourage them to talk *about* you. It's not about you talking *at* them.

As I mentioned earlier, many companies treat their Facebook fan pages like big billboards, when in reality they're more like cocktail parties. Just imagine this for a moment: You're hosting a party at your house. There's food and good conversation. People are talking and enjoying one another's company. All of the sudden a message comes over your home theatre surround sound system screaming, *"Attention! Super, sizzling, sensational, summer savings! Start the summer off right with our RED HOT 48-hour super savings special! 50% off ALL services for the Next 48 Hours!"*

Seriously, just imagine that one for a moment. Do you think you'd get people's attention? Sure you would but the outcome wouldn't be good. Your guests at the buffet table would stop mid-chew. People would be elbowing each other with that weirded-out *"okaaayyyy?"* look in their eyes. Why would anyone do such a thing at a social gathering? It sounds ridiculous right? Sure it does, but that's how a lot of businesses are using social media these days. They're actually driving people away by treating it like just another advertising medium, like TV or radio. Then they wonder why their click-through rate is dismal at best.

Now imagine the same cocktail party where the guests are all raving about what an amazing job the caterer has done. One guest takes the catering company's business card for their daughter's upcoming wedding. Another guest hires the company for their next corporate event and a third guest wants the catering company to handle their 50th birthday party next month. That my friends, is what "Social Marketing" has been like for years, and the Internet has not changed it. It's simply provided a new and more powerful, far reaching place for word-of-mouth marketing to take place.

Bottom line: If you want to engage the promoters in this new social media marketplace you have to ditch the "interruptive marketing" and make it a social process. This means when someone asks you if you're doing social media marketing you no longer just respond by saying, *"Um… Yeah. We've got a Facebook page and a Twitter account."* Instead, you have to be able to say, "Yes, we're engaging with our customers in the *conversations* taking place on Facebook and Twitter. We're using our customer generated content (raving reviews) and other social capital to create high quality content."

**POWER** TIPS

*Connect your Facebook fan page to your Twitter account so that each time you repost a customer's comment about your company or a raving review from a review site as your status, it instantly goes up on Twitter.*

*What you want is your fans and your followers to see messages from your customer instead of from your company.*

When I say get it and get on it "ASAP," I really mean, "ASAP." This isn't happening next year or next month. It's happening NOW! People are talking. People are listening. You are either leveraging your social capitol to increase sales or waiting for a slow death that is costing you valuable missed sales opportunities.

**85%** of consumers say they are more likely to open their wallets when they can find online recommendations to support offline advice.

**89%** of consumers declared they find online channels to be trustworthy sources for product and service reviews.

**87%** of consumers agreed that a favorable review has confirmed their decision to purchase a product or service.

(Source: Online Influence Trend Tracker, Cone Communications, 2011)

To amplify things, consumers are faced with the same challenges in our difficult economy and they aren't taking any unnecessary risks. Consumers can't afford to purchase services from a dud company only to regret it later. They now have more time than money and are doing their research before they make any buying decisions.

It only takes a few seconds for a prospective customer to look up your company on Google. If you have a bad rap they'll not only see that right away, but they'll see a list of your best competitors on the same page. If you're not focused on being remark-*able* before you focus on marketing then your marketing dollars could end up driving your customers to call your competition! (Your competitors will love you for that.)

The good news is that the reverse is also true. If your reviews sell your company, you could end up reaping the reward of your competition's advertising investment by intercepting their would-be customers.

In other words, the market isn't ruled by the company that spends the most money on advertising or the one that shouts "We-We-We" the loudest. It's ruled by the company who best leverages digital word-of-mouth marketing.

This will happen whether you like it or not so you'd better start taking part in the conversation. Your customers don't need your permission to write an online review or post a negative comment on Facebook for all of their 450 friends to see. If a customer has a bad experience with your company and decides to post a negative review on Yelp, the Yellow Pages site or any other similar review site, they will, and you can't stop them.

With Twitter, it works differently but can often yield the same (if not stronger) results. For example, a prospective customer can search all tweets that have been directed to a company. It's as easy as entering that company's Twitter handle into the search bar at the top of the customer's Twitter homepage. When they conduct the search, their timeline will be filled with everything that has ever been said about that company from other Twitter users. No filter.

If someone had a great steak at Morton's they may tweet "just had the best steak of my life, thanks @mortons." However the opposite can be true as well. Someone just getting off a terrible flight may say "@jetblue has the worst flight attendants." It's all out there on the timeline, for anyone to see. Any one of your customers has the power to start a flurry of posts/tweets about your company; do you want them coming from dissatisfied or happy customers?

If you happen to have an unsatisfied customer, it's your job to respond to them promptly and appropriately. Whether it's a tweet back, a call, or a written response to an angry Yelper, you have the power to control your online reputation. If you don't help build that reputation, it will get built for you *by default,* and most likely by the person who has not-so-nice things to say about your company. We all know that unsatisfied customers are much more vocal than satisfied ones.

This is why you need to get obsessed with not only *earning* five-star reviews, but also with getting them in front of the customers who are looking for services your company provides. Sitting idly by and letting your customers define your company without you is no longer a viable option.

With just a sentence on an influential review site they have the ability to take away business or bring new business.

I don't want to get into too much detail here, but the new rules require you to (1) tell your customers right up front that their needs are important to your company, and (2) after the job is done, ascertain their level of satisfaction — simply ask them when the business is over if they are satisfied. If they aren't, do whatever it takes to satisfy them — within reason — *before* they go off bad-mouthing your company.

So now that you have a clear picture of where we are and how we got here, let's talk about where things are headed in the very near future and why we-we marketing will become even more irrelevant than it is today.

# Is SEO Truly Dying?

You may have heard the term "SEO is dead." It's not quite true. What IS true is that SEO is now different, very different. There are some very important stalwarts of SEO that remain. You still need good content, relevant page titles and an easily searchable site for the Google search programs to read and index your online identity. But many of the strategies of the past flat out don't work anymore.

Many of these over-optimized strategies are on life support and becoming less and less relevant as a stand-alone marketing strategy. Too much content or back links will hurt your rankings and in some cases, get your site banned. In fact, the recent Google Penguin algorithm updates specifically targeted sites which were "over-optimized" with keyword heavy content and with back links which were deliberately built by the site owner.

Strategies such as mass back-linking, two-way linking, and mass directory submission no longer do the trick (pun intended). Tricks do not work anymore, and search has changed.

While I'm not here to give you a lesson in SEO, it is important to understand how your online reputation and your directory listings play into search.

# The Rebirth and the Future of SEO

In the past, content and incoming links were the secret weapons of SEO, but it's important to understand *why* backlinks were so important. To Google, a backlink was a popularity vote. It meant that someone thought your site was interesting and relevant enough to link to it. Of course, this wasn't always the case since SEOs soon discovered that they could make their site appear more popular by building links.

Why could they get away with this? Because Google's technology wasn't advanced enough to measure popularity "votes" using another method. Social Media accounts changed all that. Now, a share on Facebook or on Google+, a Tweet or a Facebook like represents a popularity vote. In most cases, these "votes" can be traced back to a real account and a real person. Of course, there are still ways to fake this, but for how long?

The only thing standing in the way of UGC and social votes completely replacing link building and even causing sites building backlinks to be severely penalized is that Google can't completely track the source of a backlink.

Do you want to take a gamble that this will be the case forever? It won't, in fact some things are already starting to happen which suggest that traditional "type in this keyword and get these results" searches will no longer be the primary shopping method for digital-age consumers.

# How is Your Google Real Estate?

As you already know, location is a key component to the value of real estate. If you own property on Park Avenue, it's more valuable than property on Skid Row. Now, think about that in relation to your "Google Real Estate" or the value of your company. You can find your Google Real Estate by typing in your company name followed by the word "reviews." The results that come up will give you an idea of your online property value. Is your business on Park Avenue or Skid Row?

When someone "Googles" your company name, it's as if they're driving by your business. Do this the next time you're online and ask yourself what kind of "curb appeal" you have online.

Good? Great? Average? Poor? Nonexistent?

Most business owners aren't thinking about the Internet in terms of owning property —either high value or low value. They still think of the Internet as something on their computer, when in reality the Internet is quickly becoming just as relevant as the physical street you drive down looking for a bricks and mortar store to make a purchase. To get an example of what I mean, let's do a little experiment.

Do a search for a service that would almost assuredly require a local company i.e. a plumber, dry cleaning, dining out etc. You will find three things on the Google results page:

(1) Advertisements (PPC ads)

(2) Google+ Local (usually including reviews).

(3) Organic search results (starting below Google+ Local)

When presenting these three things, Google wants to return the best and most relevant possible results for every search query typed into their search engine.

Since the Google local search results come up first, reviews are crucial to getting your company name in front of the customer *without even scrolling down the page.*

This is not only true when it comes to listing in Google+ Local, it's also true in your organic listings, which many times don't start until the local results end. The further down users have to go, the less likely they are to connect with your company. That's how your Google property value impacts your local results.

## Beyond Local, Organic SEO

Organic SEO has changed. In the past, if you ranked first, you got clicks. Now, that first organic listing might not even show up until you scroll down past the local and sponsored listings.

However, what about those times when a Google maps section does not get displayed? How about when they sneak organic results above the maps section? This happens quite often. What sites are showing up then?

Well if you have a tremendously optimized site, then hopefully your site shows up. However, more and more, Google is 'sending' searchers to third party review sites. They are taking over our 'first pages' and pushing down the smaller, more static sites. You can use this to your advantage.

To reiterate, Google is very secretive about their algorithms and how they rank. If you look at what sites are showing up for your relevant keywords, you will see less of your competition, and more third party review sites. This is great news for you, because your company is about to embrace being obsessive about customer service. This will convert to bolstering your online marketing.

Think about it, instead of paying for your site to be optimized, you can raise your business to the cream of the crop on sites that get *millions* of hits a day. You can do this by focusing on providing stellar customer experience, and reaping the benefits of your happy customers raving about you online.

It makes sense to focus energy on improving how you are perceived on third party review sites. Not only are they getting a large chunk of the search real estate, but they also get *direct traffic*. Numbers show that simply coming up first in a search engine result is no longer a guaranteed phone call. Consumers are doing their own research — and here is where the term "SEO is Dead" may make a little sense — you may have a great website that attracts visitors, but remember that getting business is less about what you say and more what others are saying about you.

Google has long used trust as one of the factors they take into consideration when ranking websites. They factor in the trust they have in websites linking to you, the amount of social mentions you have, the length of time your website has been operable, etc. They want to send their users to companies that are the most relevant and trusted.

Now there is a new measurement of trust and Google is paying attention. Reviews: The perfect way to get real information on companies, the perfect combination of marketing and trust. They want people to not only find great companies on their organic search engine, but they also want users to find out about great companies using their paid sponsored ads within their search engine.

## How the New Rules Affect Old SEO

Not too long ago Google came out with the "Penguin release" and according to Ken Krogue of Forbes.com this Penguin "is a code name for the algorithm that decreased search engine rankings of companies who were using schemes to artificially increase their rankings. Google decided to change the weight of their emphasis from "backlinks" and more towards social media likes, shares, tweets, reddits, and 1+ (Google's obvious favorite.) In the world of digital media the emphasis is on follows, comments, and views as well." (Source: *The Death of SEO: The Rise of Social, PR, and Real Content*, Ken Krogue, Forbes.com, July 20, 2012)

 CLIMATECH **HEATING & COOLING**, INC.

7087 Campground Road, Denver, NC
(704) 483-7343 · climatechnc.com
**30** 40 reviews
service tech · technician
"David was on time,very organized and performed the check up quickly and ..." - judysbook.com

Ⓑ Lakeside **Heating & Air Conditioning**
4394 North Highway 16, Denver, NC
(704) 483-4273
2 reviews
"Always the best!" -

Ⓒ Southern Comfort **Heating** and **Air Conditioning**
Denver, NC
(704) 200-8222

Ⓓ Climatech **Heating & Cooling**
Denver, NC
(704) 489-8866

Ⓔ Safe Way **Heating & Cooling**
7067 Hunters Bluff Drive, Denver, NC
(704) 661-8688

Ⓕ Ferguson **Heating & Cooling**
195 Raceway Drive, Mooresville, NC
(704) 799-3297 · ferguson.com

Ⓖ Larry's **Heating & Air Conditioning**
Brawley School Road, Mooresville, NC
(704) 664-8050
"Found Larry's name here on Yahoo and since his business was near my home, ..." - yahoo.com

Keep in mind that today there's more than one form of search results. First, you have the old style organic search results that list web pages like yours. Now we have the local business search results that are tied to Google Maps. When you type in a service category such as house painting, along with a location such as Denver, NC, Google understands that you're looking for local services and shows you a list of local companies along with pins on a map indicating their location. These listings also include a link to the company's reviews and an average rating with a maximum of 30.

When you click on one of these local links, they don't go immediately to the company website. Instead, they take you to a Google Local + listing with more information about the business. If you claimed your listing, added relevant content and information about your company, and created a company that naturally wins reviews, then your listing will show up higher in the search results than a listing with no owner, no content, and poor or non-existent ratings.

For convenience, a list of ideas for improving your SEO can be found at: SMBRbook.com/seo

Other trusted recommendation sites are following Google's lead and trying to give shoppers the most useful information possible. Very soon, if you have a bad online reputation you won't be found in top results on search engines *or* directories. In fact, some trends in local search are beginning to reveal that you need to take more than just Google into account when it comes to your search engine rankings.

## Modern Trends in Local Search

Web 2.0 exploded by the middle of the first decade of the $21^{st}$ Century. However, in order to find a good service company, you still had to sit at a desk and thumb through a search engine or two and browse a bunch of websites. With the advent of recommendation sites like Yelp and with all the work that Google is putting into its local search features, even your website is now becoming less relevant. Bing is also using Yelp to add credibility to their local search results just as Google is using the reviews placed on Google Places through Google+ Local. Reviews are taking over local search, and at the time of this writing, the same trend is taking over global search as well. Let's look at some of the present trends in online search.

## How Directories Can Take Traffic AWAY from Your Website

In the early days of online directories, each listing consisted of a short description (usually pulled from a website's "description" meta tag) and the title of the page with a link to the website. It wasn't much better than the Yellow Pages. In fact, it could be even slower because companies could fit a lot more information on a website than in a Yellow Page ad, forcing you to rifle through multiple web pages to find the same information that was included in a Yellow Pages bullet list.

Not anymore! If you haven't already, I suggest you surf on over to Bing.com or Google+ Local and take a look at the state-of-the-art online local service directories. Just tell them what you're looking for and where you're located and they'll present you with a list of local service companies with map locations.

You'll also notice that ratings and reviews have a prominent place on these listings! Each listing contains an average rating and an ongoing log of customer reviews. If a business listing has been claimed by the correct company it will also have a bulleted list of services, maybe some photos and videos, hours of operation, and often times some kind of coupon or special deal. Each listing is a one-page "Cliff Notes version" of your website.

There's no need to wander off the site and skim a half dozen websites to make a decision. *Often times you might as well not even have a website as far as a Yelp user is concerned.* There's something even more important going on here than just the fact that your customers are contributing the bulk of the content to these pages via reviews. Your competitors are *advertising on your Yelp listing!*

*Not Cool!* But very clever. If a shopper sees low ratings and bad reviews for your company they have another choice staring them right in the face! That's like paying for dinner only to watch someone else sit down and eat it. You would *never* allow your competitors to place ads on your website, right? Well, it's not your site so you have no choice in the matter.

So now you know that sites like Yahoo Local and Google Local and review sites such as Yelp are circumventing your website with their abbreviated version of your business, there's another trend going on. If you thought the last one was big you're in for a walloping surprise with what's coming just around the corner...

## Intelligent Mobile Apps Are Replacing Computer Browsers

Did you know that the iPad by Apple is one of the fastest selling electronics products in history? What about smartphones? They were the first truly personal computers. In fact, mobile market research firm, Canalys, estimated that 158.5 million smartphones were sold in the last quarter of 2011, compared with 120.2 million personal computers. What these statistics are telling us is mobile marketing will undoubtedly replace traditional computer browsers for online searches. Why wouldn't it? More iPads, more smartphones and less PC's mean desktop searches will be the exception and not the norm.

With the iPhone, came the "app" – a self-contained computer program that you could launch with the touch of a finger. Apps from websites like Google, Yelp,

Superpages and others now allow consumers to *connect* directly to service directories. This enables them to see ratings and reviews and make decisions without ever having to use a browser, navigate a search engine, or ever read a single web page! But it still doesn't stop there! Now the apps are becoming intelligent!

## The Rise of the Machines: Intelligent Assistant Apps

By the end of the last decade a company called Siri was working on a new service directory app — one that you could *talk to*. Siri was also a new kind of search engine. It can tap into and pull information from a long list of service directories and other online resources, gathering all the information together in one place.

Today Siri works in conjunction with Yelp to help you find local services. But the major difference is that when you "talk' to Siri it recognizes your verbal request to help you conduct a search without typing a single word. Even text messages aren't really "text" messages anymore; they are transcribed and sent from your audio command.

Siri is also tied into companies that provided actual services such as purchasing movie tickets, calling cabs, and making restaurant reservations. With this technology you can set up a dinner-and-a-movie date, make a restaurant reservation, and call a cab all by uttering a sentence or two.

When it comes to searching for a service, Siri is a breeze. A shopper can say to Siri, "My house has termites," and Siri will reply with, *"I have found several extermination companies relatively close to you,"* and then present the user with a list of extermination companies including ratings, reviews and distances from your location. In the time it used to take someone to open up a web browser and type in "www.yellowpages.com," a Siri user is already looking at a list of service companies and deciding which one to call.

People naturally become addicted to anything that makes life easier, so you can bet that once this starts it will become popular very quickly. Without having to spend time reading a website, is it any surprise that app-enabled smartphones and mobile tablet computers like the iPad are being used more and more?

## Welcome to the Future of Service Marketing

Today, the power to make or break your company is literally in the palm of the consumer's hands. It's clear to see what's going on now, but where is this all leading in the future?

Recommendation sites, AI and voice recognition such as Siri are quickly becoming more sophisticated and advancements will proceed at a very rapid pace. The next step beyond AI assistants of today is for them to actually start making decisions for us. In the near future AI assistants will be better than humans at determining which of the service companies in a long list of contenders is the *best* choice.

Computers are already better than humans at picking stocks, diagnosing diseases, predicting weather, finding legal precedencies and much, much more. Choosing a good service company is a trivial matter compared to these complex fields. How will they do this? These unforgiving AI agents won't be looking at bullet points and cute photos in Yellow Page ads. They won't care how good *you* say your company is. They won't care about the content on your website or how well it was optimized for search. They won't care if the Bud Girls are at your location signing footballs. They will rely on one thing and one thing only. Can you already guess? They will rely on customer experience and user generated content!

## It's Time to Change the Way You Think about Marketing

So you now know what a lot of business owners and even some professional marketing consultants are for the most part oblivious to — that reviews, ratings, and online content created by the public are more important than any content you can generate.

Yes, times are changing fast and it's nearly impossible to keep up with all the new technology. You're better off focusing on the principle which is quickly taking over marketing, the same principle which Pepsi leveraged when they created the Pepsi Challenge. Consumers now have a voice, and that voice is louder and more influential than billions of dollars' worth of we-we marketing.

For service companies, online marketing is nearing the pinnacle of its evolution. All of this technology which has been evolving over the past 20 years is leading to one place: five-star excellence in service is becoming the new marketing. Eventually it will be so quick and easy to find out who's naughty and who's nice in the business world that people will have very little thinking to do.

If you're like most business people, just the thought of Internet marketing, social media and SEO is intimidating. You already have employees to manage and a customer base to tend to. You don't have time to worry about Facebook, Twitter, Google, search algorithms, back-linking and all those confusing new terms, acronyms and the technologies of the Internet.

The fact that customers now have all the power online can actually be empowering for those of you who are feeling overwhelmed by the constant need to adapt your marketing plan to changes with online technology. It is good news to those of you who have been shoveling out several hundred (or several thousand) dollars a month on SEO to rank your site at the top of Google.

If you earn great reviews you will be way ahead of your competition without having to be a super Ninja Internet marketing expert. Just remember, the bad guys have to rely on paying to manipulate rankings — for as long as they can afford to pay or for as long as they don't get caught, which they will. Good guys that take care of their customers and have a solid marketing strategy are destined for greatness. As the saying goes, "the cream always rises to the top," so be one of the good guys and you will swiftly float to the top.

# Chapter Two Summary:

1. With Web 2.0 customers went from having no power to having the power to do more good or bad for your company than you could ever do yourself, no matter how much you spend on Yellow Page ads, direct marketing, SEO, blogging, PPC ads and so on.

2. If you want to create a raving fan club (your social capital) and you want to make your competition green with envy, you have to understand the principles of socially-driven marketing.

3. Many companies treat their Facebook fan pages like big billboards, when in reality they're more like cocktail parties.

4. The search engines are rapidly applying strategies for making the online world more social and more trustworthy. To stay on top of the game (and the search pages) your company needs to be on the same page with the search engines and the review sites.

5. Google is now incorporating reviews from Google places into local search results. They're also requiring people writing reviews to have authentic Google+ accounts. Bing has teamed up with Facebook and Yelp to incorporate social dynamics into search results and reviews into local search results.

# Chapter 2 Recommended Reading

*Landing Page Optimization: The Definitive Guide to Testing and Tuning for Conversions*, Tim Ash (Sybex, 2008)

*Social BOOM!: How to Master Business Social Media to Brand Yourself, Sell Yourself, Sell Your Product, Dominate Your Industry Market, Save Your Butt, ... and Grind Your Competition into the Dirt*, Jeffrey H. Gitomer (FT Press, 2011)

*The Ultimate Question 2.0 (Revised and Expanded Edition): How Net Promoter Companies Thrive in a Customer-Driven World*, Fred Reichheld and Rob Markey (Harvard Business Review Press, 2011)

*Trust Agents: Using the Web to Build Influence, Improve Reputation, and Earn Trust*, Chris Brogan and Julien Smith (Wiley, 2010)

*Word of Mouth Marketing: How Smart Companies Get People Talking*, Andy Sernovitz (Greenleaf Book Group Press, 2012)

# Chapter 3

# Rule 2: Power Your Profits through Remark-*ability*

The first step to exploding your word-of-mouth marketing is to get serious about what it takes to make it happen. You have to become "buzz-worthy" and you do this, not through better marketing, but through delivering a remark-*able* customer experience.

TARGETED **TIPS**

NEW RULE:
Remarkable service
is the new marketing.

I know some of you are probably wondering what customer service has to do with marketing, selling and making money. It has everything to do with it, because remarkable customer service *is* the new marketing.

Which begs the question…

## Are You Socially Trusted Online?

By now you know that positive reviews, User Generated Content (UGC), Google+ votes, and recommendations on highly influential sites such as LinkedIn, Facebook and Yelp all demonstrate high quality trust signals. So do interviews on credible news channels or featured articles in newspapers or other types of print media increase your credibility and social proof. These are all ways consumers use to resolve their personal insecurities about which businesses to use. The more loyal customers you win and the more social signals your company accumulates online, the more confidence a consumer will have about choosing your business over the competition. But that's just online right? Oh no…far from it.

There's a filter through which all your prospective customers will pass your company before they even consider doing business with you. That filter is how socially trusted you are according to your online reputation, and it doesn't matter if that customer found you through an offline or an online marketing channel.

For example, imagine you spend $10k on a TV, radio ad or a direct mail campaign. Your customer sees the ad, they're interested, but they don't buy yet. Instead, the first place they go is Google. They want to find out what people are already saying about your company. Do you think it will matter how persuasive your TV ad, your direct mailer or your radio ad is once your customer has read what other consumers are saying about you?

Even money back guarantees don't have the impact they used to when it comes to getting more phone calls or online leads. After all, why should someone take you up on your offer to "try it out risk free" when it only takes 30 seconds and the help of Google to pull up several reviews on your company before wasting their time or giving out their credit card number?

Offering the lowest price isn't much better. People still want to know what other consumers are saying. With only a few clicks they can see a comment or review that suggests they won't get the value they're looking for from you.

When I say your online reputation impacts the effectiveness of your marketing, I'm not just talking about the effectiveness of your *online* marketing campaigns. Every type of marketing you do will be passed through the "Social Filter" of your online reputation.

## Who's Really in Control of Your Online Reputation?

Hiring *ethical* reputation management companies or online marketing companies while offering poor or even mediocre customer service is like trying to put perfume on a pig. You can cover up the smell for a while, but in the end, a pig is a pig. Unhappy customers are notorious for being more vocal than happy customers, so if you have even a few unhappy customers, you can bet it will impact your online reviews.

You can dump tens of thousands of dollars into online marketing and reputation management services in an attempt to push down or bury your negative reviews (aka "manage" your online reputation) but you're ultimately trying to control something which isn't under your control. Your online reputation is in the hands of your customers.

That's the bad news. The good news is, unlike your online reputation, your relationship with your customers *is* under your control! When you build a great relationship with them and win positive reviews online, your online reputation will amplify every other kind of marketing you do. In essence, you can take control of turning your clients into co-branders and promoters.

To better understand how to build those great relationships, let's take a look at the three types of customers who can help you co-brand your business.

## Three Kings of Online Consumers

Dell Computer is a classic example of a company who "got it" and started taking part in the conversation. Their brand image was suffering as a result of not focusing on customer service and they knew they needed to engage in the conversation. They came up with their "Ranters and Ravers" campaign that allowed their customers to write blogs on their site. With this platform they gave a voice to both the Ranters and the Ravers and quickly showed the world that customer service was now their top priority.

Today's digitally empowered customers have superpowers. With just a sentence on a review site they have the power to take away business or bring new business. That's why it's important to understand all three.

# The Ranters

The Ranters are the customers who make it a point to tell the world just how much they think your company failed them. Their superpower is they can turn customers away from your business with a few keystrokes and a click. Some people are just Ranters by nature, and will only take the time to write about your company for the purpose of "getting even" with you for doing anything wrong. Some people believe companies are evil entities designed to take their money and give as little as possible. Those people take great lengths to do as much damage as they can by telling their experience on PissedOffConsumer.com or RipOffReport.com.

There will always be customers that are impossible to please. But a good portion of Ranters are people who are also willing to go out of their way to praise you when you do right by them. This can be hard to believe, so I'll show you a true story that happened in my company "1-800-Anytyme." Check out this screen shot from our company Facebook wall:

**1800AnyTyme Plumbing, Heating, Electrical, Air Conditioning**

362 likes · 9 talking about this · 11 were here

Like    Message

Heating, Ventilating & Air Conditioning · Plumber

1064 La Mirada Ct, Vista, CA,

(760) 542-6088

362

About        Photos    Likes    Map    Videos

Post    Photo / Video

Write something...

New Customer ▶ 1800AnyTyme Plumbing, Heating, Electrical, Air Conditioning
August 18 near San Diego

**BEFORE:** This company looked great in the reviews, but I was not impressed. They were late, blaming the heat for a computer meltdown. Hard for me to believe guys on the truck didn't have a schedule. Also, wouldn't give me any idea of the price for replacing a faucet on the phone, and I thought $225 for taking ours out and putting a new one we had purchased in was very expensive. Then he needed another $110 to replace water supply because it was a different size, and didn't tell us that until faucet was installed. Then took the old faucet and all the instructions for the new one without asking us whether he should. I had planned to save it and get a new hose, which was all it needed. We had company staying here, so couldn't do two days without a kitchen faucet. Won't use them again.

New Customer ▶ 1800AnyTyme Plumbing, Heating, Electrical, Air Conditioning
August 18 near San Diego

**AFTER:** Just had the most amazing thing happen: after I posted a negative review, 1800anytime showed that they really care about their business. They phoned, and I ignored it, but then a customer care rep actually appeared at our door, wanting to make things right. I couldn't be more impressed! I had complained about charging $110 for a new water supply line without informing us in advance, and they refunded that! In addition, the rep insisted on leaving a gift pack that included dinner on them, coffee and mugs, and several other amenities. Must say, we were amazed and pleased, and it made us believe they really care about their business and their customers. So impressed!

Will definitely use them again!

What you just saw wasn't an example of a customer with alter egos. The negative comment came after her first experience with us, which I'm sorry to say did not live up to our company's standards. The second comment was posted after I encouraged the customer service representative to show up at her door with a gift basket and an apology.

That's one way to turn a Ranter into a Raver, so don't say it can't be done.

We also have to remember that Ranters, whether we like it or not, serve an important purpose in the world of commerce. That's why Yelp was created in the first place, to keep companies accountable.

Although Yelp can be a thorn in the side for some companies, Yelp gives weight to people who regularly write reviews. A lot of Yelpers feel they are doing a community service by reviewing local businesses. They are not only warning people of the bad ones, but also praising the good ones. These are the Ranters you want to focus on because all good business owners know you can learn a lot more from legitimate upset customers than you ever can from the happy ones.

Most often, the difference between a Ranter and a Raver has nothing to do with the customer and everything to do with the company serving them.

## The Passives

The Passives are the people who just can't be bothered taking the time to write a review. Their superpower is with just a few minutes of their time they can save themselves and their friends hundreds or thousands of dollars by doing up-front research before spending any money.

You might never turn a Passive into a Raver, but with a little motivation you can usually get them to write a quick review. If you want to explode your online reputation, let me tell you where you really need to invest your time, money and energy.

## The Ravers: Your True Most Valuable Promoters (MVPs)

These are your ultra-loyal customers. They derive their superpowers from Twitter, Facebook and other social media. They have more Yelp merit badges than a Super Girl Scout. They have the power to turn themselves into a digital billboard and spread the buzz about your business to hundreds or thousands of potential customers.

The online raving promoters are the best kind of customers. They're the ones going out into the world shouting your praises. They'll tell their friends and family on Facebook, +1 you on Google, Tweet about their wonderful experience on Twitter, rate you on Yelp, and so on.

Certainly not every one of your customers will be a Raver, but you never know who is and who isn't until after the fact. You simply need to get into the frame of mind that you'll turn all of your customers into Ravers by blowing them away with a remark-*able* experience.

# How to Turn Ranters into Passives

Right up front I'd like to say this: After you've read this book, if you don't go and get everyone at your company on board with the idea of making customer service your top priority then I simply haven't done my job in convincing you that you don't have a choice. If you are convinced, and you start taking action, you will see the number of Ranters begin to steadily decline. Hopefully over time the Ranters will have nothing to complain about.

You don't want them to use a site like RipOffReport.com to write a bad review that will be next to impossible to remove. Your online reputation is too important to just throw up your hands and concentrate on the MVPs. Whether we like it or not, online engagement with and from the customers has put us all in the trust business and it's critical that your social proof exudes that trust and exceptional service.

Vince Lombardi is credited with giving this advice to coaches and anyone in a leadership role, "Praise in public, criticize in private." Well, in a way that is what you need to do with your customers.

It's very important, under these new rules, that you uncover those unhappy customers *before* they go off ranting about your company in public and find a way to make it better. Let them know that happy customers are your number one priority and you want to know what went wrong so you can fix it. Then make sure you publically thank them for the opportunity to right the wrong. Other fans and followers will see your status update about how you solved a problem and they will take notice of your professionalism and your dedication to customer satisfaction.

I don't want to get into too much detail here, but the new rules require you to (1) tell your customers right up front that their needs are important to your company, and (2) after the job is done, ascertain their level of satisfaction — simply ask them when the business is over if they are satisfied. If they aren't, do whatever it takes to satisfy them — within reason - *before* they go off bad-mouthing your company online.

## How to Turn Passives into Ravers

If you're getting your train on the right track then more and more of your happy, passive customers will turn into raving MVPs. There are also other things you can do to get the passives to take a few minutes and write you a review — besides just blowing them away with your amazing new customer service ethic.

Here's where we get into my "secret sauce." I don't want to give away the recipe too soon because I believe you need to read the rest of this book before you rush off and start implementing the new customer service philosophy. But the one thing I will say here is that Passives have a few concerns. One is convenience, another is motivation, and a third is privacy.

First, after you've ascertained they are happy you have to make it easy for them to post a review. Second you have to give them a *reason* to want to post a review. Third, if privacy is important to them, you have to give them a way to post a review without signing up for an account with a review site and giving away their identity or email address.

So how do you do all of this? First, give them options because what's easy for one person might not be easy for another. If you're pushing someone to review you on Yelp and they don't have a Yelp account then you won't get a review. Many people already have an account with Facebook, Google, Yahoo, or AOL (which ties into City Search). Some are signed up with YellowPages.com or SuperPages.com or some of the other lesser-known sites. Get on all of them! You should have your business listed on *every single one of these sites* plus any specific to your industry (like UrbanSpoon, TripAdvisor, and Hotels.com). Then offer your customer an easy way to access the review site of their choice. If they don't have an account with any of these sites then it will be hard to convince them to create one, but a few of the sites don't require users to create an account or give away their email address.

The real secret in the sauce is the motivation. Why would a Passive want to take the time to write you a review? If you can't bribe them, what can you do? What incentive can you offer them?

Well, if your staff has really gone out of their way to do right by them, to the point where they are simply blown away at how hard you worked to provide them with a blissful experience then you already have some leverage. If your employees have a way to politely ask them to write a review for them *personally*, as a favor and as a reward for doing a good job, then the customer is no longer just writing a review about a company but about a *fellow human being* - one that just bent over backwards to make it a remark-*able* experience.

## Do Something Special for your Ravers!

In this new age of social media your Raving Promoters are your company's single most valuable asset. You have to identify them and be extra passionate about showing your appreciation for them. If one of your customers posts a raving review on Yelp, for instance, and they never hear from you again, no big deal, right? But now imagine you are that customer. You post a raving review and the company you just reviewed follows up with a comment like this: "Thank you Jenny!! It's customers like you that let us know we are appreciated which makes all this hard work worthwhile. We love you too, Jenny!!!"

By publically acknowledging them on your social media platforms you extend the conversation, keep them engaged and you can now share their positive review with all of your fans and followers. In addition, they are more likely to tell their circle of influencers about how you reached out to them. That's the type of reputation you want to build by word of mouth. And that's the difference between using social media as your own billboard versus being engaged in a conversation with your customers.

It's not just important to treat every customer like a potential MVP. Remember the old game of saying "Next!" as you finish serving a customer? That philosophy is dead. The new game is about staying engaged with your customers and making them an integral part of your company culture and brand personality.

Now that you know how to maximize the Three Kings of Online Consumers, let's look at how successful companies have optimized their customer relationships to become leaders in their industries.

For convenience, a list of ideas on providing remarkable service can be found at: SMBRbook.com/remarkable

## How Remarkable Service Trumps Traditional Sales and Marketing

Many business owners see customer service as a type of damage control and think of marketing and sales as the engine which drives company growth. Meanwhile, successful companies like Tony Hsieh's Zappos get away with spending very little on advertising and instead use remarkable service to create mind-boggling growth. These types of companies are making one simple decision which sets them in a league of their own when it comes to creating long term success, growth and equity, making them the envy of every entrepreneur on the planet.

They're making customer-centric service their primary product and therefore, their primary marketing strategy. Early adopters of customer-centric service will turn raving fans into effective online promoters. They won't need to come up with out-of-this-world, Thomas Edison-caliber products or marketing ideas in order to create explosive sales and company growth. Their very business will become its own advertisement.

In 2003, when Zappos was going through the roughest financial period of their early years, Tony Hsieh made some cuts (in between fundraising rounds) in places many experts thought would certainly cripple Zappos' growth. Rather than continuing to spend a large amount on advertising, Tony did something completely out of the ordinary and decided to cut most of their advertising and marketing budget. He shifted those resources and invested them in creating a remarkable customer experience. As it turns out, this act of supposed "entrepreneurial suicide" catapulted Zappos' growth and revolutionized the way businesses were being run. After making that groundbreaking decision, Tony grew Zappos from $70 million to $184 million over the course of just 12 months. (Source: *The Zappos Experience: 5 Principles to Inspire, Engage, and WOW*, Joseph A. Michelli (McGraw-Hill, 2011)

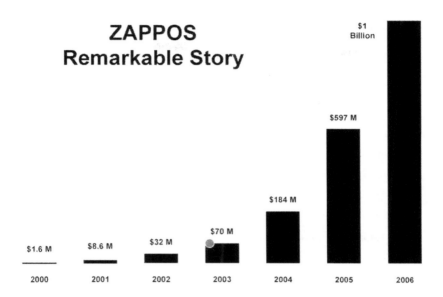

**ZAPPOS
Remarkable Story**

| | | | | | | |
|---|---|---|---|---|---|---|
| $1.6 M | $8.6 M | $32 M | $70 M | $184 M | $597 M | $1 Billion |
| 2000 | 2001 | 2002 | 2003 | 2004 | 2005 | 2006 |

Over the next few years, Zappos continued to grow, going from $184 million to over $1 billion dollars in sales. This total growth from only $1.6 million to $1 billion took less than ten years.

Now here's a question to consider... Is there anything earth shattering about selling shoes?

If you were to slip and fall in the shower, hit your head on the toilet and come up with the idea to sell shoes online, would you charge out of your house and run wet and naked down the street screaming: *"Eureka, Eureka?"* Probably not. Selling shoes wasn't a remarkable, innovative, or outstanding business idea. If shoes were all Zappos had to offer, they'd have been priced out of the market by monster companies like Amazon and other online retailers who were willing to simply offer a lower price.

For convenience, a list of resources provided by Zappos Insights can be found at:

SMBRbook.com/zappos

So how did Tony Hsieh grow Zappos so big so fast? He did it through remarkable customer service and turned ordinary satisfied customers into raving promoters and brand ambassadors who shared their positive stories through some of the largest social recommendation platforms on the planet.

## Making Remark-*able* Service an Obsession

In an August 14<sup>th</sup> 2011 article by Cotton Timberlake, published in *Bloomberg Business Week,* it revealed that the high-end retail store, Nordstrom, grew by 12 percent, reaching $9.7 billion in the year 2011. Meanwhile, the Great Recession slowed the growth of Nordstrom's rival companies such as Neiman Marcus and Saks. Nordstrom sells mostly clothing, which again, isn't a remarkable or innovative business idea.

What is it that got *Bloomberg Business Week* (and their millions of readers) to take notice of Nordstrom? Remarkable customer service. Nordstrom considers customer service to be their primary product. Their confessed "secret" is Nordstrom has no CEO and is not run as a corporation with only a group of investors making decisions. Instead, Nordstrom is a family-owned and operated business which is dedicated to providing a remarkable customer experience.

The extended Nordstrom family owns the same kind of paper as any other shareholder. They claim their goal is to preserve the integrity of the business by continuing to put the customer first instead of profits. They aren't exploding through some genius marketing or branding strategy, but they are expanding slowly in the U.S. and taking the enterprise to places in the Middle East and Asia.

How did Nordstrom, a high-end clothing retailer, grow during a great recession, when people could have chosen to save their money by purchasing clothes from Macy's or Bloomingdale's? They did it by making customer service their primary product and doing it in a remarkable fashion.

## How Remarkable Service Made People Fall in Love with the Big Apple

Few success stories are more remarkable than that of Apple Computers under the leadership of the late Steve Jobs. Apple is one of the biggest success stories, if not the biggest, of the U.S. economy in the past few years. They're now the highest valued U.S. company even over Exxon/Mobile. In fact, in June of 2011 Apple had an even higher operating cash balance than the U.S. National Treasury!

On the surface, Apple's amazing success seemed to be linked to innovations such as the iPad, iPhone and iTunes. Everyone has hailed Steve Jobs for his foresight in mobile technologies and many have even called him the "Thomas Edison of our time." But what you probably didn't hear about was that one of Apple's biggest advantages over competitors like Microsoft was their innovations in customer service.

Steve Jobs was obsessed with creating a remarkable customer service experience. In his book *Letters to Steve Jobs*, author Mark Milian shows us dozens of emails from the inbox of Steve Jobs. Many of these emails are correspondence between Steve and his customers. While they do reveal many of his imperfections, they also demonstrate that Steve Jobs wasn't the stereotypical Techy Geek hiding from his customers behind a brick wall of administrative assistants who screened his emails. Instead, Steve Jobs, the CEO of one of the world's most prominent technology companies, had direct contact with his customers.

But Apple's dedication to creating a remarkable customer experience doesn't end there. When so many people are choosing to shop online, Apple is still bringing in the retail business based on the way the customer feels in their stores. In a recent article on TheSocialCustomer.com, Andy Hanselman claims that more people visit Apple's 326 stores in a single quarter than the 60 million who visited Walt Disney's four biggest theme parks in the year 2010!

Apple's marketing secret isn't some persuasive, hypnotic copywriting or celebrity endorsement. Their "secret" is they created a remarkable customer experience just like what you learned about in Chapter One. The Apple stores have intensive training programs for employees; programs which are focused on creating a customer-friendly culture and store atmosphere.

These customer service guidelines were taken directly from playbooks written by Steve Jobs. They included: intensive control of how employees interact with customers, scripted training for on-site tech support and consideration for every store detail right down to demos, photos and music preloaded onto mobile devices.

They even have their own app that allows customers to check themselves out when making a purchase. So no more standing in line or waiting for a representative to ring you up. You simply scan the product code using your own iPhone and pay through your phone.

Their primary reason for doing this was to consistently deliver a remarkable customer experience. Surprisingly, the employees at Apple stores are also advised *not* to sell, but to help customers solve problems. As one training manual states:

*"Your job is to understand all of your customers' needs — some of which they may not even realize they have..."*

A recent article in the Wall Street Journal included the Apple acronym which the customer service agents were trained to follow:

# A.P.P.L.E.

**A: Approach customers with a personalized warm welcome.**

**P: Probe politely to understand all the customer's needs.**

**P: Present a solution for the customer to take home today.**

**L: Listen for and resolve any issues or concerns.**

**E: End with a fond farewell and an invitation to return.**

(Source: "Secrets from Apple's Genius Bar: Full Loyalty, No Negativity," Wall Street Journal, June 15, 2011)

Meanwhile, Apple's primary competitor, Microsoft, experienced much less success when they opened their own similar service stores. Their company growth, in comparison to Apple's, has also been less significant.

## Being Remark-*able* is the New Marketing

Today trying to grow a business through marketing alone is like trying to eat Cornflakes without the milk? Not exactly the breakfast of champions. The same is true when you spend money on marketing but deliver only average or satisfactory service to your customer? It just doesn't work.

But in the age of digital word of mouth, being average, or even good, in the customer service department is no longer enough to build a successful business. You can increase your marketing budget until it exceeds your total revenue and you'll still never see the growth you would if you spent resources on creating a company culture entrenched in exceeding customer expectations and winning reviews. If you're only offering mediocre service, customers will not feel inspired to write a great review, and even more will be put off by being *asked* to write one.

Providing remarkable service is a whole other ballgame. Rather than focusing solely on costly marketing campaigns to bring in potential customers, make providing great customer service and teaching your employees how to win reviews the priority. As a result you'll have a successful combination that will grow your business and more importantly you will start to see the profits you deserve.

The most amazing thing about remarkable customer service is that the more competitive your market becomes and the tougher things get with the economy, the more important and valuable being remarkable becomes.

Any company that offers a decent product and who has a reasonably good marketing strategy can grow when the economy is booming and consumer confidence is high. But it takes more than "good" marketing to grow a company when the economy is bad and when competitors are snarling at your door, ready to pick off your prospects and customers. Here's why...

## Remarkable Service "Stops the Bleeding"

Remarkable customer service is the only cure for the hidden menace causing your business to hemorrhage money. That menace is customer turnover and a lack of online and offline conversions which will continue to bleed your resources as you struggle to earn new customers.

Lack of customer loyalty is a bigger problem than most business owners realize. This is because many of us are too busy trying to keep new business coming in the door. But the moment things get a bit dry with the economy or a new competitor enters the picture, the "running to keep up" becomes a frantic sprint.

Prices get slashed, people get laid off, and budgets needed to buy new equipment or to create new training and incentives for employees, disappear. In the meantime, the business owner is getting nervous that the phones aren't ringing; the trucks aren't moving and customer walk-ins are getting scarcer.

Meanwhile, companies who create a remarkable customer experience are getting most of their business from repeat customers and from referrals generated by existing customers. These companies have very little to fear from a dip in the economy or from a new competitor entering the picture. They've created an experience which converts their customer base into a tribe of loyal followers and an enthusiastic sales force.

We all know that getting new customers is a lot of work. It takes time and money. Sometimes, it takes a lot of money. However, for most companies, keeping those customers coming back instead of going to the competition is even harder. Today's marketplace has become so competitive that customer loyalty seems nearly extinct.

The reality is, in an attempt to cut costs, companies have chosen automated voice systems, FAQ pages and poorly trained, outsourced customer service agents in place of good old-fashioned, live support. However, if you create a company in which a remark-*able* experience is the overarching principle you are on your way to more loyalty. In other words, *customer loyalty is in direct proportion to a company's commitment to providing remark-able customer service.*

If you want your customers to be 100 percent loyal, you don't have to be the lowest bidder. You only need to be loyal to them by delivering a remark-*able* experience every time. Remarkable customer service stops the bleeding of customer turnover and could literally save your business in a tough economy.

So what do I mean by "Be Remark-*able*?"

## Remarkable Means "Remark-*able*"

Just think about the word "remarkable" for a second. It literally means to be "remark-*able*." Want to know if you're company is operationally sound in the service of your customers? Just ask yourself what type of remarks you're getting. If you're getting a lot of great comments about your company, so many that you can fill several web pages with your positive customer reviews, you're exceeding expectations to the level that the customers' are willing to talk about it.

If you're not, then you've yet to tap into the awesome power of remark-*ability*. On top of this, you probably have more customer turnover and reduced repeat business and referrals than you realize. Your golden goose might even be on life support.

That's the reality. No matter how great you think your customer service is, if you aren't getting rave reviews you still have work to do. Becoming buzz-worthy is all about *customer buzz,* not company buzz. Let's look at some essential dos and don'ts for offering remarkable service.

## The ABCs of Being Remarkable: The Story of "Quick and Easy Quentin"

Our story begins on an ordinary day at an ordinary factory. Things were fine at the headquarters for Ted Jones, the owner of a large TV manufacturing plant; that is, until one of his conveyor belts stopped working!

Within seconds, his entire operation was backed up. Ted started to imagine piles and piles of money going up in smoke. Panic set in as he scrambled through the Yellow Pages. That's where he found an ad that read: "Quick and Easy Quentin! Fastest wrench in the West. All your machine problems solved FAST so you can start making money again!" That clinched it for Ted. He made the call and within 20 minutes, Quick and Easy Quentin wheeled into Ted's parking lot, rising from his truck like a genie from a magic lamp.

Although an expert in repair for more than 20 years, Quentin sure didn't look the part when he showed up at Ted's shop. Quentin was dressed in a greasy T-shirt and a ragged pair of tennis shoes. His hair looked like a cross between a toupee and a wet mop and his breath was bad enough to take the paint off a car.

Needless to say, Ted wasn't thrilled with his first impression of Quentin, but considering his production line had come to a screeching halt, he figured he didn't have the luxury of being picky about his appearance.

Just a few minutes later, after tightening a small screw on the underside of Ted's machine with nothing more than his 4-way screwdriver, Quick and Easy Quentin had Ted back in business. Then it came time for the bill. $250.00 for Quentin's service. Ted was furious!"$250.00! You were here for 5 minutes! I want a breakdown of these charges!"

With that, Quentin got a bit irritated. To make his point, Quentin grabbed the bill from Ted and wrote out his breakdown.

Task T-1000: Tightening of 1 ¼ screw: $1

Task T-1001: Knowing which screw to tighten: $249

Of course Ted understood the point Quentin was trying to make, but he couldn't justify it in his mind. As far as he was concerned, guys like Quentin should never be able to make that kind of money per hour, especially not walking around in dime-store tennis shoes and a greasy T-shirt. Jones paid the bill while mumbling under his breath with disgust, then sent the fastest wrench in the West packing. And of course, Quentin received no review to show future customers, no pat on the back. Nada.

Quentin felt unappreciated, as he should. He'd been punished for being a fast and efficient expert and for expecting to be paid just as much as an amateur who would've taken the entire day to find and fix the problem.

Have you ever felt like Quentin?

You can spend countless years and hundreds of hours training, all the while investing money and elbow grease into learning your trade, only to have your value judged by the amount of time it took you to do the job? But Quentin made a big mistake. He did the job well, but he missed the ABCs of being remarkable.

Had Quentin known his ABCs, Ted would have happily paid him the $250 and sent Quentin out with a positive review and an invitation to the annual company barbeque and softball game. The ABCs of being remarkable can do the same for you and your team. They'll also help you settle what has come to be a common debate in the world of customer service...

## To Wow or Not to Wow? Winning the "War of OR"

During my time in writing this book, I ran into some seemingly conflicting information between the Zappos approach of wowing the customer and the philosophy of Harvard School of Business who said that wowing the customer should not be the number one priority. Who would ever assume that wowing the customer *isn't* the first priority?

According to the smart folks at Harvard, the number one priority should be to *solve the customer's problem.* Keep it simple and don't try to go over the top. I've had experiences, as I'm sure you have, where a company was trying too hard to get me to like them rather than focusing on solving my original problem. On the other hand, it's the going above and beyond which makes a company truly remarkable and creates an unforgettable experience for the customer. So which is it? To wow or not to wow?

The answer is it's both!

The tricky part is making the two concepts work together by creating a seamlessly remarkable experience from start to finish. This is where the ABCs of being remark-*able* come in. So let's take a break from Quentin's story and I'll share with you how the ABCs work in today's world of influential review sites.

## The ABCs of Remark-*ability*

## A - Always Give Your Customers What They Need First

Customer service starts with giving people what they need. This is the foundation of being remarkable, if you don't do this first, nothing else you do will matter. Sounds simple, but since it's not common practice, it doesn't come so easily for a lot of us. As I mentioned just a minute ago, doing the job and confirming that it was done right needs to happen before you start putting bells and whistles onto the experience. It's like if you're eating at a restaurant and your steak is incorrectly cooked, you don't want the waiter to refill your drink, cut your steak, sauce it and wipe your mouth when you're done. You just want your steak cooked correctly...do the basics right first.

Customers make positive remarks about those who exceed expectations when it comes to meeting their need to be heard and validated as human beings. Just as you can wrongfully assume you understand someone's problem, so can you wrongfully assume their expectations were fulfilled. You can't always depend on them to tell you when you missed the mark either. In fact many times people just settle for good enough, only to turn around and tell their friends about the "half-ass" job you did.

Seeking to understand someone's problem, and verifying with them that you understand, sets a clear expectation. To build trust, you must fulfill that expectation and confirm it has been fulfilled and the job is complete. Again, sounds simple, but have you ever hired a service person who didn't complete the job to your satisfaction?

What if they walked out of your house believing they did do a good job? If you never said anything to them and they never asked, the expectation might never get met. How likely is it for you to leave a positive review in that case? Not very. This is why as a service provider you should never simply assume your job has been done correctly.

At 1-800-Anytyme, we believe a job is never done until the customer says it is. Part of a good customer service plan is to confirm that a job has been fulfilled according to the expectations set in the beginning. Without this you could ask for a positive review and the customer will think to themselves, "Well, I would have been glad to give you a review if you would have just gotten it right from the start and listened to my instructions better."

They might even speak up and tell you the job wasn't completed to their expectations. Better to confirm this first and to give yourself an opportunity to fix it before you even THINK about asking for a review.

In fact, this first step is so important that I'd suggest you treat the following steps, such as earning and asking for the review, as if they didn't even exist until the first step is completed. It's like finding a drowning man out in the water, your first job is get the life preserver around his neck and get him to shore. Once you get him there, you can offer him a towel, some hot chocolate, and a free coupon for swimming classes. But until you get him on dry land, those bells and whistles need to stay out of sight and out of mind.

Respect, trust, and validate that you've heard and understood your customer's needs: all of these will build a relationship which will make it easier for him/her to recognize that you're paid based on your expertise, even though you may have spent little time fixing their problem.

## B – Be Remark-*able*!

Meeting the basic needs of your customer isn't enough to make you or your company remarkable. Customers must be blown away; so blown away that they can't wait to tell the world. Merely satisfying your customers isn't enough if your goal is to turn the volume up on your word-of-mouth marketing by earning scores of positive online reviews.

You probably already know how hard it is to get a customer to write a review. I know, I've seen business owners go through it. They go to a marketing seminar where someone sells them on how important reviews are, gives them the vague advice of, "get customer testimonials," and then leaves them hanging without specific details on *how* to do this. They get pumped up and start asking for customer testimonials. They get maybe one review for every one hundred they ask for.... and the review looks like this:

*"Great service! Thanks!"*

Okay, that's one positive review. But after a few weeks of begging and getting almost no responses, the business owner gives up, and the employees are no longer following through on asking for them. Within a few months, the initial buzz generated by expectations of a flood of positive reviews is gone. What happened?

You've given good service, respected your customers, listened to them, and fulfilled their expectations. So where is this mountain of great reviews? Well, you didn't earn them, because you didn't create a remark-*able* experience. I know, pretty harsh right? But let's be honest, it's difficult to wow people these days. We have 72-inch flat screen, High Definition TVs and home theatre surround sound systems in our living rooms that make the movie theatres our parents sat in look pathetic.

We have access to just about any information on any subject at the tip of our fingers. We have Google, Twitter, Facebook, and YouTube. We have Six Flags, Disneyland, Disneyworld, and Discovery Cove. We have voice recognition Android applications, text messaging, webcams, iPods, iPads, iPhones, laptops, netbooks, and tablets. Not to mention cups of coffee priced at $7 with more ingredients than a seven-course meal.

We are spoiled consumers, and that means we're damn hard to impress. This is why you can't just deliver customer satisfaction, ask for a positive review and get one. You have to put the cherry on top by absolutely wowing your customers.

Again don't forget, you must meet the customers' primary needs first. If you don't do this, trying to go above and beyond could backfire. Instead of a positive remark, you'll blow your shot at getting them to come back, and you might even get a negative review because of it.

For example, have you ever been to a restaurant where the waiter or the waitress delivered lousy service, but tried to "butter you up" just as they were bringing you the check? Maybe they brought you enough mints to give you a mouthful of cavities. Maybe they gave you a free dessert, or they were just extra nice to you in hopes you'd leave them a decent tip. It's obvious, it's disingenuous and it won't encourage you to leave a big tip.

How do you blow your customers away once you've met their needs for respect, trust, and validation and fulfilled the service for which they initially hired you?

Chances are you already know how to do this. You just need to get creative and start paying attention to their needs. If you learn to listen and pay attention, you'll find plenty of opportunities to rise above and deliver truly remarkable service. Here are a few examples of what it looks like to create the kind of experience that deserves a winning review.

At ReviewBuzz, we have a coach named Ramon Morales who worked for 4- and 5-star hotels where he was the head trainer for customer service. His guidance to the staff was to make the guest more than just happy, they wanted to inspire them to tell the world about their amazing experience and become lifelong raving fans. To get a sense of how dedicated Ramon is to exceeding expectations, let me share a real-life story with you. Ramon had a customer who didn't like the steak they ordered from the hotel restaurant, and while most service professionals would have offered either to replace the steak or give the customer his money back, Ramon went above and far beyond what you could ever expect. He ordered a steak from a competing restaurant across the street and personally delivered it right to the customer's room. You can bet Ramon received a great review and the customer asks for him during every repeat stay.

In his book *Delivering Happiness,* Zappos CEO, Tony Hsieh tells a story about how one of his friends called the Zappos shoes customer service number and asked the representative to help him find a local pizza delivery service that was still open at 2 o'clock in the morning. Most companies would have dismissed the customer's request and turned the call into a company joke about the "stupidest customer requests." But the Zappos representative did exactly what the customer asked. Before you shake your head at this, remember that excellence in customer service was the primary factor responsible for Zappos growing to over $1 billion annually in less than ten years.

If it's not obvious yet what the key to remark-*able* service is, it's remark-*able* employees. Exceptional employees are not hired, they are created. They are provided the tools to do their job well and given the autonomy to go above and beyond without checking in with a manager for approval. They are clear about their boundaries with company procedures but they understand their main focus is the customer. They love receiving positive feedback and they are competitive with themselves and others to be the best, under any scale of measurement. But I will share more on how to make that happen later on.

For now, let me just give you some insight into how over the top Zappos representatives would go to provide an amazing customer service experience. Here's a real email sent to a Zappos customer whose shoes had fallen apart:

Mail Inbox (4,952 Messages)

**Re: Recently Ordered Shoes (Order 113884488)**

From: **Zappos.com** cs@zappos.com          Date: **Sat, Dec 3, 2011 at 10:12PM**

To: _____

Hello _____

Thank you for contacting the Zappos.com Customer Loyalty Team. My name is Paul and it would be my pleasure to put a smile on your face today! Those shoes are falling apart on you?! That is unacceptable and I am so sorry for that! Luckily for you, I was recently in an experimental lab explosion involving a lamp, a giraffe, and an expired pack of Bazooka bubble gum. As Captain Anomaly, I now have some totally awesome WOWing power that I can use to take care of this for you!

**KAPOW!**

Whoa! What was that?! Look closely, do you see it? If I use my super vision, it appears to be a message from your back statement. It says that in the next 2-10 business days, as soon as your bank authorizes it, you will see a credit of $89.99 from Zappos. But why?! Because I have refunded you in full for those shoes since they have fallen apart on you so quickly.

**WOOSH!**

Oh gosh! Did you witness what just took place? Quickly, look to the inbox of your e-mail. You should see a few e-mails from us, but one of those will contain a link to your pre-paid UPS return label! Just put that first item back into the original packaging and tape that new label on the outside with clear tape. If you do not have a shipping box, any plain, unmarked cardboard box would work fine.

**BLAMMO!**

Holy smokes! What could have occurred just now?! I have used my laser vision to vaporize that poor customer service experience, and have created a coupon for you to help mend your online experience wounds in this troubling time.

That coupon is for $15 and is a one time use, non-refundable coupon that can be used on your next order within 90 days. Please accept this as a further apology for what has happened. The code to use that coupon is below for your convenience.

As for the shoe, we do not have it in stock any longer, which is why I could not teleport a brand new one to you. I would assume it was probably a fluke defect on that one particular item, but either way I apologize that this has happened.

I certainly hope this help. If you need anything else, please do not hesitate to let us know and we would be glad to assist you. I will even fly down there to handle that for you myself! Permitted that I am not busy saving kittens in trees, of course. Captain Anomaly, awaaaay!

**Thank you very much!**
**Paul**
**Customer Loyalty Team**
**Zappos, Inc.**
**Contact us 24/7, 365!**

Even if you don't have customer service superpowers or plan on helping your local pizza delivery joint find new customers, you'd better start asking yourself how you plan to put the icing on the cake and roll out the red carpet for your customers.

All your team members and managers must know and understand the importance of reviews. Everyone in your company should know how to earn one and how to request the type of review the customer will gladly take the time to write. Everyone should know why they, as a company, must become proactive about generating reviews and the consequences of not doing anything about it.

## C - Create Value from Start to Finish

By now you've heard me talk a lot about creating an experience for your customers. I know, it sounds like Yoda telling you to simply "use the force," doesn't it?

But what I'm talking about is creating an experience that will help your customer feel secure about the value they're getting in exchange for the price they're paying. Quick and Easy Quentin didn't do this. He was more concerned with being fast and efficient (and possibly wanted to hurry to his next job or even his lunch break). Had he spent more time doing just two things, the entire story might have gone differently and he probably would have earned a raving customer review from a very easy job.

First, he could have educated his customer better. Robert G. Allen, the author of *Multiple Streams of Income*, nailed this one when he said:

*"No matter what your product is, you are ultimately in the education business. Your customers need to be constantly educated about the many advantages of doing business with you, trained to use your products more effectively, and taught how to make never-ending improvement in their lives."*

It's also been said that the cure for fear is education. Okay, so it might not help you overcome your fear of going scuba diving with sharks on the Great Barrier Reef with a raw steak around your neck, but it will certainly help your customers feel better about the money they're paying.

Quentin could have used his decade's worth of expertise to educate the customer about the problem and the solution and thus increase the customer's perception of his value. For example, why did he pick that particular screw and why is that screw so important to the operation of the machine? He could have talked about all of this while Ted Jones was still riding the high of having his machine up and running again. How long would it have taken? Just five minutes? Educating his customer might have also helped him sell another service or a second visit.

He could have been proactive with his expertise as well. If you want a good example of this, go to an auto dealer and visit their service department. Sometimes you go in there wanting to have your windshield wipers replaced and they call you in telling you that you need new brakes, a carburetor flush, an oil change and an air filter.

While I'm not encouraging you to upsell your customers on every service imaginable, I am emphasizing that there's a lot to be learned from the proactive approach they take. Imagine 'Quick and Easy' Quentin checking the other machines in Jones' manufacturing plant, tightening them up and doing a few proactive things free of charge, the whole time letting Jones know what he was doing and why he was doing it. Imagine Quentin going above and beyond solving Jones' problem by working to prevent similar problems from occurring in the future. After all, if you're going to charge someone $250 for less than an hour of your time, what can it hurt to spend a few minutes creating value for free? For instance, what if he asked a few more questions about how fast the machine was operating and advised Jones that he could speed up its efficiency and increase its lifespan just by a few routine check-ups? Heck, what if he'd just asked: *"While I'm here, are there any other funky things happening with these machines?"* Or... *"How else can I help while I'm here?"* Or... *"Since I'm here, how about we also check out your____."*

What goes in the blank for you? Your expertise gives you insights into how to improve your customers' lives in ways they didn't even think were possible. You know how to save them time and money and you can spare them from emergencies and the added cost of a service call. Don't assume you're putting yourself out of future work by doing this. On the contrary, you're building trust with them, and you never know when they might say: *"Wow, I didn't know I needed that, let's take care of it while you're here."* If you educate your customer and offer proactive advice or services, you'll create an experience the customer will not only remember but will want to share with others.

To put this into perspective, think about your last trip to Disneyworld, or even the last time you saw a great movie. Or how about the last time you paid nearly $6 for a regular size non-fat extra foamy latte? It wasn't just the latte you were paying for, it was the experience. In all of the above settings, hours and hours of work and creativity went into creating an opportunity to immerse you in a positive experience.

Great care is taken to keep anything from entering the experience which might break the spell. Many high-end, five-star restaurants use music, lighting and decorations to create an experience. Movies use sounds, lighting and visual effects to create an experience. Of course, you might not be taking your customers into a mystical journey of romance and imagination like the guests at Disneyworld or onboard a Mediterranean cruise. The point is that a remarkable experience is *seamlessly* remark-*able*. From beginning to end, every action builds value on top of value until the customer is absolutely blown away.

This begins with the first impression. The way you start a customer relationship sets the standard for the entire relationship. It's almost magical the way this works. Your job is to create as many amazing moments between you and your customer as possible. Just think about how much weight we give to first impressions.

Why are first impressions so damn important to us? Isn't it because your first impression of someone sets the standard for how you perceive them and therefore how you treat them? Likewise, when you make an initial impression as a person of value, you set yourself up to be treated that way.

In fact, by making the right first impression, you can eliminate 90 percent of the drama which would have otherwise followed in the weeks, months, and years of that customer relationship. It's the same thing when you're connecting with prospective customers. How customers treat your company and your employees is 100 percent determined by the way they perceive you. If you establish yourself as a person of high value and someone who can be trusted, that's how people will treat you. High value people expect excellence and they have a low tolerance for B.S., this is why they get treated well.

The bottom line is that low-value behavior, including negative feedback, is created by making low-value impressions, both in the beginning of the relationship and when the work is finished. And of course, that also translates into potential loss of profits.

High value first impression = premium fees = more available resources to deliver high value services = more probability for good reviews = more high value first impressions = more premium fees = even more available resources to deliver high value services = even more probability for good reviews = even more high value first impressions = even MORE revenue and profits.

You can end up foiling your first impression if you don't have a strong follow up, or if someone catches on that your first impression wasn't genuine. But people are funny; they don't like to be wrong. If their first impression of you is that of a high value, you have to mess up pretty badly to get them to admit that they were wrong about you in the beginning. In fact, sometimes you have to mess up quite a few times. But if you make a low value first impression, it's an uphill battle from there. Hell, many times you won't even get the chance to undo your first impression. In addition, by giving a low quality impression you set yourself up for them to haggle with you about rates, ask for additional favors without being charged, and even mistreat your employees.

Value is also created when companies listen well and understand customers' needs and take care of them with forethought. In his book *The Seven Habits of Highly Effective People*, Stephen Covey talked about "seeking first to understand and then to be understood." This is some of the best advice for making a good first impression on prospects. You can also be the smartest and most knowledgeable expert, with solid gold insights that will make drastic improvements in the quality of your customers' lives, but until they feel understood your customers could care less about what you have to say. Bizarre, but it's so true. Being remarkable is not just about being great at what you do, it's about building great customer relationships...and you're probably already better at this than you realize.

At my company, 1-800-Anytyme, we have specific practices for creating a great service experience from start to finish. They are nothing magical or earth shattering, in fact, they're really easy to do. Unfortunately, they're also easy *not* to do.

If we revisit the story of 'Quick and Easy' Quentin you'll remember this is where poor ole' Quentin went wrong. He could have worn a professional uniform, an ID badge, a clean and shiny pair of work shoes, combed his hair and gulped down a box or two of breath mints before meeting Ted Jones.

At 1-800-Anytyme professional appearance is expected of all our sales and service representatives in order to create a higher value experience for the customer as well as to reassure them about who is coming to their house. Remember that when you're in a service-oriented business, your *people* are your primary product.

Your customers are already sold on the service you provide, and if they see positive reviews online, they're already pretty close to being sold on your company. Now, it's simply a matter of selling them on *who will perform the service*, and this has little to do with your company credibility. For instance, if you've ever looked up a local website to get a sports massage, you probably read about their company mission, what type of massage they provide and their hours of operation. You know that when you go there you won't have previous knowledge of the individual therapists so you won't know who to ask for. But what if you could see the photos of each therapist, with their areas of specialty AND customer reviews about them specifically? That takes the guesswork out of choosing the company as a whole and the best individual therapist for your needs.

We all know that even a good company can have a few bad employees. So when you're sending a representative out to a customer's house, you need to sell that person just as you would any other product.

At my service company we highlight each employee through our email confirmation system. When an appointment is set, we collect the customer's email address and send out a detailed profile of the representative. This profile includes the professional picture as well as a detailed explanation of the person's training and experience *and* a list of personal reviews from his customers. I'm not talking about a photo I took of our tech in the break room, all sweaty from a recent service call either. I'm talking about a professional quality photograph, like you see below.

We are not only showing the company in a good light, but we are featuring our employees because we are proud to have them as representatives of our brand. By highlighting our staff we make them feel valued while also giving the customer peace of mind. We know this is important to our customers because the Meet Our Crew page of our website is our most valuable real estate page. It's the most popular page with the most viewer time logged in according to our analytics.

By sending the confirmation and introduction of the representative, we're also being proactive on two fronts. First, we get the email address without the awkward concern from the customer about whether we're going to blow up their email inbox with spam. Instead, we're asking for the email with a specific purpose in mind…we want to ease the customer's concerns about who will be visiting their home. Second, and more importantly, we make life SO much easier for both our customer and service personnel.

In addition, when we enter a customer's home, we wear floor protectors to keep from tracking dirt inside. We show up in complete uniform: jacket, hat and polished black boots, clean tools and a clean tool bag. We greet the customers with a warm and friendly smile, we listen to their problem and we work on building a relationship *from the start*. We also bring a reusable, environmentally friendly grocery bag as a gift, which goes a long way towards establishing a great first impression and creates a bit of reciprocity that we can leverage later. When the technician is finished, he verifies with the customer that the job is done before the invoice is presented. Lastly, we provide our technicians with new towels and company-provided cleaning supplies so they clean up after themselves, making sure they leave the customer's house just as clean as they found it.

If Quentin had taken the time and forethought to do these steps when he visited Ted Jones, how different do you think the $250 bill incident would have gone? What if he'd been quick and easy about performing the service, but taken his time in building the relationship and presenting himself to Ted?

The most important point in all of this is that you're *not just selling your services.* You're selling yourself. That's the primary product for anyone who is involved in the service industry. I can buy carpentry, massage or chiropractor services from anyone who has the capacity to do a great job. But as you know, most of us don't just buy from anyone. We buy from someone who we know we can trust to treat us right. Quentin did a great job of selling his services and a poor job of selling himself. That's what made all the difference. Applying the ABCs in your business starts with accepting this responsibility and practicing it throughout your company.

The primary product is YOU.

The bottom line here is when it comes to creating a remarkable service experience it's all about the relationship with the customer. Relationships aren't built quickly and easily, they're built by careful attention to detail and by treating people so well they'll be happy to write a great review for you even before you ask for it.

## Are you using the ABCs at your company?

Remember…

A: Always give your customers what they need first

B: Be Remark-*able*

C: Create value from start to finish.

I want to stress here that you have to make the ABCs an absolute, must-do priority for everyone in your company. You have to become obsessed with wowing your customers, especially those who could become your MVPs (Most Valuable Promoters).

There was a time when you could just be a 'Quick and Easy' Quentin, and a lot of service companies are still doing it that way. But times are changing fast and so is the market. If you provide a great customer experience through the ABCs of remarkable service, people will talk about you. They'll tell their friends and acquaintances how well your company treated them. Now that they're doing this online, hundreds, even thousands of people can and will read it. Your happy customers will become like walking billboards and will literally help co-create a powerful and attractive brand. They'll step over your competitors to get to you and they'll encourage everyone they know to do the same. If you make the ABCs a habit, you won't have to be the cheapest in town, because people will pay you a higher fee to be treated well. In fact, a 2011 study by comScore for EXPO Communications found that customers were willing to pay over 30 percent more to a company with excellent reviews.

 The million dollar question is: Will she recommend you and write you a review or not?

That's the question to ask, and if you want a positive answer, it's time to get busy becoming remark-*able*.

The personal reference has always been a powerful marketing tool, but today it's becoming a necessity. It's the secret for those who want to stop marketing and start growing and making serious profits.

Will you be one of the early adopters of being remark-*able*? If so, you have to make winning and collecting positive reviews just as much a priority as the collecting of money in exchange for services. Today your service teams need to know that providing remarkable customer service is a duty, not a choice. This also applies to the step-by-step system your company creates for delivering remarkable service and for collecting customer reviews.

If you want to be the Zappos or Apple of your industry than you need to start thinking and behaving like Tony and Steve. They were both on the front line of customer service and did more than create a business they created the ultimate customer experience. You have to ask yourself what that means to you. How can you stay engaged with how your customer is treated throughout the entire experience with your company? What would make it easier for them to find you, hear about you, do business with you and then spread the good word to others? You have an opportunity to be the next Zappos or Apple if you pay as much attention to the details as you do to the bottom line.

Do this, and you'll start to realize that the bottom line grows because of remarkable service. That's where the next, and perhaps the most exciting, rule comes into play.

# Chapter Three Summary:

1. Being Remark-*able* IS the new marketing.

2. Every type of marketing you do will be passed through the "Social Filter" of your online reputation.

3. When you build a great relationship with your customers and get them to post positive reviews online, your online reputation will amplify every other kind of marketing you do. In essence, you will turn your clients into co-branders and promoters.

4. You should have your business listed on every single social media site, review site and directory, plus any appropriate industry-specific sites such as TripAdvisor or Hotels.com. Then offer your customer an easy way to access the review site of their choice.

5. Everyone in your company should know how to earn a review, how to request a review and how to motivate customers to write a high quality review.

6. Ravers (MVP's), Ranters and Passives all need to be treated differently in order to coax them into behaviors that will translate into buzz for your company.

7. Always keep coming back to the ABCs of marketing. It's the proven way of being remark-*able*. Are you using the ABCs of marketing at your company?

# Chapter 3 Recommended Reading:

*Delivering Happiness: A Path to Profits, Passion, and Purpose*, Tony Hsieh (Business Plus, 2010)

*"I Love You More Than My Dog": Five Decisions That Drive Extreme Customer Loyalty in Good Times and Bad*, Jeanne Bliss (Portfolio Trade, 2011)

# Chapter 4

# Rule 3: Turn Reviews into Revenue

I want you to take a trip with me into a world where every one of your marketing campaigns is a slam dunk. I'm not just talking about new sales, I'm talking about the four "legs" of successful marketing:

For convenience, a list of ideas for marketing with reviews can be found at: **SMBRbook.com/marketing**

*Imagine: More New Prospects*

What if you could nearly double your amount of calls from new prospects?

*Imagine: More Sales*

What if *every time* you ran a campaign, you were almost *guaranteed* to make sales?

For convenience, a list of ideas for selling with reviews can be found at: **SMBRbook.com/selling**

*Imagine: More Money Per Sale*

What if you increased the amount of money earned per sale?

*Imagine: More Referrals Per Customer*

What if you could increase or even double the amount of referrals?

What if there was *one thing* you could do to get all of these working at their full potential?

I know this sounds unlikely. But I'm about to show you how it's more within your reach than you think.

Imagine having an ad, a flyer, a website or a PPC add that converted a guaranteed percentage of its viewers. This might not be possible using graphic design and copywriting alone because there's always some degree of uncertainty in any sales approach. But with authentic reviews, you have a much better chance of taking the uncertainty out of your marketing and advertising. Let that sink in for a moment, and think about what that could mean for outselling your competitors.

To show you exactly what I mean, let me introduce you to a real-life success story of how reviews impact *every aspect of your marketing and even your offline sales.*

## How Chris Raspino Became a Sales Superstar

Until now I have explained the importance of remarkable service and earning quality reviews. I have even highlighted some very well-known success stories. That's all great, but what about your company? How can you apply these principles to your industry and transform your business? Perhaps this real-life example of a service industry professional will help to put it all into perspective.

Chris Raspino, a salesman from Stuart Services, earned almost 30 positive reviews, all five-stars, in 60 days, and became more socially trusted to his prospective customers as a result. If you're anything like me though, you're probably wondering what the tangible benefit was to Chris' business.

Simple:

1. More leads from new prospects

2. More leads turning into sales

3. More money per sale

4. More referrals through reviews.

No matter what industry you're in, if you master new connections, new sales and maximize your value per sale and get customer referrals, you're undoubtedly firing on all cylinders. Most companies dump a ton of money into those four things, yet a single solution can solve all of them, just as it did for Chris when he solicited the help of my company, ReviewBuzz. As I mentioned in the Introduction of this book, ReviewBuzz combines the strategies of leveraging customer service operational expertise, post sales marketing tools and review leveraging to optimize visibility and credibility for service industries.

When Stuart Services started as a client with ReviewBuzz, they were spending a lot of money on their website and their Facebook page but they weren't seeing any significant results from their efforts. The problem was, they were "off the grid" when it came to winning buzz and building trust signals. Not because they weren't giving great service, but because they had no way of proving to potential customers they were socially trusted by their existing customers. If their prospective customers went to their site or their Facebook page, they'd see information about the company and how to contact them, but that was it.

They had previously tried using a company-produced portfolio including pictures of the clients and the job. Yet, they only collected a handful of testimonials, all on comment cards instead of on trusted and influential review sites. Testimonials on comment cards might as well be invisible in today's age of social media.

## How Social Trust Increased the Amount of New Customer Calls

Within the first 60 days of using ReviewBuzz, Chris earned and won 27 exceptional reviews on highly influential review sites from real customers, all mentioning specific benefits of using Chris and his company. What does that mean to Chris' business? Anyone looking for his services would see the social trust he established and choose him over his competition. That equates to more leads, more sales and potentially more reviews to keep the cycle of increased brand awareness in motion.

Now imagine you're looking for a service professional online and a Google search brings up 50 reviews, all with five-star ratings. When you look at the reviews themselves, you can't help but notice the majority of them are for a guy named Chris. Meanwhile, there are five other companies, with either no reviews, mediocre non-personalized reviews or no recently written reviews. Who would you be more likely to call? This is how Chris accomplished the first part of the formula – more leads from new prospects.

As for the next challenge — more leads turning into sales — that was practically a done deal. When you have social trust, people don't just call to check you out and settle their fears about who you are and whether you're going to do right by them. They pick up the phone as a result of seeing solid reviews. Their fears are already ninety-nine percent settled. Now it's just a matter of setting up a day when the service person can come out. Under any other circumstances, there would be a long list of questions about who was coming out to the house, and the persistent, nagging fear about whether or not they could be trusted in the customer's home. Trust signals from popular online recommendations sites erase those fears. In fact, Chris told us the social trust gained through the reviews made their marketing collateral (website, brochures, etc.) into "just another place for the customer to get the number so they could call and set the appointment."

When Chris showed up at the door with a big smile on his face the customer was once again reassured and said, "I've seen your online reviews, you're Chris." By developing social trust, not only did Chris' sales calls increase, but when he showed up for the calls he was recognized by new customers which instantly created trust and a deeper personal connection.

Okay, so he got famous. Big deal, right? Actually, there's a whole lot more to it than that.

## How Social Trust Cuts Through the Clutter

Social trust gets the customer to call and it makes the appointment a slam dunk, but let's talk about what happens after that. As you know by now, the service experience needs to end in a remark-*able* experience for the customer and the collection of a positive review.

New client relationships come with a lot of skepticism about professionalism as it relates to industries such as home service providers, child care, etc. and many companies spend a great deal of time working through the clutter of mistrust just so they can solve the client's problem. Because of the customer's many concerns about trust, quality and fees, all the sales training about upselling the customer and increasing the value per sale becomes just a theory. After all, how can you add value and make recommendations when you're spending your energy overcoming objections and convincing them that you *can* solve their problem?

However, when you have dozens or even hundreds of customers saying you're the best, you get to skip the skepticism and objections that come with a new client relationship and cut right to the process of adding value.

Increasing your value per sale becomes as easy as selling a tall glass of ice water to a man stranded in the desert.

This is exactly how Chris increased his value per sale through leveraging social trust. Chris admitted that when he first started with our recommended process of asking for a well-deserved review, he saw it as an inconvenience to make the customer do something above and beyond writing a check. You probably have similar concerns and I don't blame you. The last thing you need is more red tape and hoops to jump through. But what Chris found is the social trust that came from having positive reviews on popular review sites allowed him to skip the most frustrating and time-consuming obstacle of all: establishing himself as a trustworthy individual and settling the customer's general fears of purchase. When those walls come down, you can start focusing on creating solutions and adding value.

This is when the advice about upselling and making additional offers actually starts to make sense, and that's how Chris used his dozens of reviews and high ratings to increase his per sale average. His confidence level also went up when he saw that his customers appreciated him more. And

No one can sell you better than your customers can sell you.

it was written all over the Internet. Most importantly, becoming socially trusted created a new expectation for

Chris to deliver the same remarkable service that had produced his list of reviews.

The process of earning great reviews is a positive cycle that starts with a sense of increased accountability to provide great service which leads to a new level of confidence of being rewarded and recognized. It's a cycle that naturally motivates you to become, and to stay, remarkable!

**Build Trust**

**Get Reviews** _____ **Drive Sales**

So that's three out of four so far: new leads, leads turning into sales, sales turning into bigger sales. All that's left now is repeat and referral business.

# Online Referrals vs. Offline Referrals

Let's assume you get an offline referral that converts into a sale and your company makes a profit. Would you trade that referral and profit for one great online review? Think about that for a second. The review might not make you a profit right away, but it will give you something far more important and valuable. Equity.

The primary difference between the referral and the review is that an online review creates equity and ongoing cash flow. It can be seen for years by dozens of people who have never met one another, referring new business for as long as it is visible in the virtual marketplace of the internet.

Essentially, an online review is a referral you can cash in on over and over again. The reach of an offline referral is limited to the number of people the referral source knows and with whom they feel comfortable enough to make a recommendation. However, one single review on a highly influential site such as Facebook or Google+ Local lives infinitely on the web and is visible to all their friends and connections. One review could easily be seen by everyone who searches for your company online.

An online review is equity, and I'm willing to bet that a time will come when standard business valuations are based on their online reputation. The great thing about this is, unless we have an Internet ice age that wipes out all the world's computers, the content on the Internet doesn't have an expiration date. That one positive experience with your company is a *permanent part of your brand.*

So there you have it, the sales power of online reviews:

1. More leads from new prospects
2. More leads turning into sales
3. More money per sale
4. More referrals through online reviews.
5.

As they say in the infomercials, "but wait, there's still more…"

## Bonus Benefit: No More Buyer's Remorse

You might think buyer's remorse only affects your sales when the buyer asks for a refund or posts a negative review. But buyer's remorse also costs you in repeat business. If someone feels horrible after spending money on your services, for any reason, do you think they'll come back? They'll go to your competitor instead. This may seem irrational, but when it comes to money and what we deem to be "fair," being rational isn't always part of our decision-making process. People need to feel that they've gotten a fair amount of value from the deal. This is how buyer's remorse causes a customer to take their business elsewhere the next time, even if they don't ask for a refund or complain. But once the person has written and posted an online review, they confirm to themselves that they got a good value for the money that they spent.

Chris also saw the effects of delivering exceptional service because his customers had less buyer's remorse when the new customer relationship started on a good note and ended with a positive review. After all, if someone has written you a review about how awesome you are, they're not likely to go back on their own word. Writing the review "seals the deal" in the customer's mind and when someone knows deep down that they've received something valuable, price becomes a non-issue.

Now what other sales and profit strategies do you know of that can solve those five key marketing challenges in one sweep?

## Imagine: More New Prospects

You know how valuable first impressions are in marketing. Do you know where you get the chance to make a first impression with most of your customers? That's right, on Google. Your first impression on Google has a staggering impact on your search for new prospects.

A company that makes a great first impression on Google will have instant credibility with Internet shoppers. That credibility will translate into greater call volume and more leads.

On the other hand, a bad first impression on Google will do just the opposite. The phone will be so quiet you'll wonder if it's even plugged in.

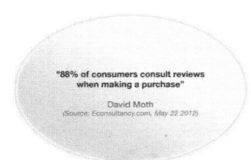

When 88 percent of customers consult online reviews can your company really afford to make a bad impression?

So what creates a person's first impression of your company on Google?

It's simple. Just ask yourself what people see when they type your company name into the Google search bar. Better yet, what do they see when they type in your company plus the word "reviews"? Example: "Dave's Auto Repair Shop Reviews"

## Do they see this?

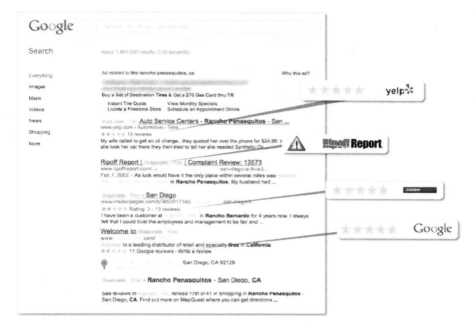

## Or does it look like this?

What a HUGE difference. These are searches consumers perform every day.

With the increased popularity of review sites, consumers are looking for the reviews of businesses or products, and not just from one site. It's no surprise that each of the examples above have the website of the company followed exclusively by review sites. Google knows that consumers are looking for reviews, and its Google's job to give people what they want.

If you know how to be remarkable, you can get a lot of these high-scoring reviews on your Google+ Local page. They are attainable. You just need to be remarkable to get them! Of course, more prospects doesn't always equal more sales, but when you've got positive reviews working for you, the sales are a slam dunk...

## Imagine: More Sales

When the economy shifts and business growth slows down, most companies can't aggressively market because they're clinging onto every dollar. This is why many business owners are reluctant to spend money on marketing, and their business stagnates as a result.

But picture this...What if your website landing pages, your advertisements, and your directory listings "aka Google Maps" all had a high conversion rate? It would be almost impossible to go wrong.

When you *know* ten percent of the people who land on your website will become customers, sales and profits will literally take care of themselves. In other words, let's assume you earn $100 from each new customer. So if you get 100 visits to your site you can pretty much bank on getting more new clients. That equates to $100 multiplied by 10 clients, or $1,000 in revenue. Conversions are the *single most important metric in marketing* because when conversions work, everything works. Even if you're paying $5 for every visitor and your conversion rate is ten percent you will not only be able to *predict* your return on investment, you'll be able to count on it.

How confident would you be about growing your company by investing more time, energy and money into marketing if your sales conversions were guaranteed? When sales conversions are high and consistent, you can rule your competition by spending money where you know you have a favorable Return On Investment (ROI). If you have an improved ROI with one method (PPC) you will feel more comfortable pushing the lever. As long as your return is profitable – keep pushing and outperforming your competitors!

Now consider that *online reviews are the key to improving your online conversions and I bet you're ready to start collecting some reviews.*

I know what you're probably worried about … *"Mike, aren't you just saying this because you're in the Review Business?"* Yes, I do own a review management company but I own one for a reason. You see, I used to be all about driving in the leads, and I still am, but my entire approach to marketing has changed because of the discoveries which led me to write this book. Here's how obvious this is when you know where to look.

## The Secret Ingredient to Explosive Growth is "Hidden in Plain Sight"

In his book *Good to Great*, author Jim Collins revealed some of his findings from studying the most successful companies in the United States. His research uncovered startling realities which break down the popular beliefs about what it takes to grow a business.

One of his key findings was that companies who experienced explosive growth were willing to face the grim realities of why their business was no longer growing and what needed to change. If your company is stuck or if it's not growing and making new sales like you want it to, I bet you a dollar I know the true reason why. It has nothing to do with marketing. It's your ability to turn great customer service into reviews and to turn reviews into powerful marketing tools.

I was forced to face this truth myself, but only after I'd been wronged by online marketers and consultants who didn't want to face the facts that conversions are dependent on more than just slick advertising. They're also heavily dependent on a company's reviews and ratings, and when I discovered this for myself, I realized that remark-*ability* (reviews) had become an essential ingredient in my marketing recipe.

I hate seeing inexperienced or less-than-honorable marketers take advantage of hardworking business owners by selling them flashy, ineffective advertising services. I'm not judging all marketers here; there are plenty of great ones out there and plenty more who are well-meaning, but not well educated. But well-meaning doesn't always mean capable and competent. Unfortunately, many of these consultants have more dollar signs in their eyes than they have years of experience under their belt. They also have more desire to make money than they have desire to gain accurate knowledge. That's a bad combination, especially when you're the one being asked to write the check for their services.

Fancy advertisements have their place, but if customers can't find current online recommendations about your company, even the best advertisements are about as good as a screen door on a submarine. Just think about this from a consumer's point of view, would you rather see "we-we" marketing or up-to-date real reviews on a trusted recommendation site?

Today's consumers are too well informed to spend their money without first finding out what their friends or *other* consumers are saying about a company. Don't let the traditional business advice fool you either, customer service and sales are more closely linked than most people make them out to be, especially today. There are some bad consultants who will talk only about sales and marketing as a means of growing a business, all the while treating customer service as a completely different subject; an afterthought, a reaction to disgruntled customers rather than a proactive, overarching philosophy.

*Being remarkable is the "hidden in plain sight, but hard to face"* **secret** *of sales and company profitability.*

# Numbers Don't Lie, Marketers Like "Chip the Cheat" Do

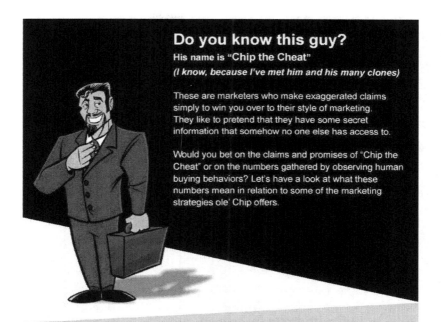

## Do you know this guy?
**His name is "Chip the Cheat"**
*(I know, because I've met him and his many clones)*

These are marketers who make exaggerated claims simply to win you over to their style of marketing. They like to pretend that they have some secret information that somehow no one else has access to.

Would you bet on the claims and promises of "Chip the Cheat" or on the numbers gathered by observing human buying behaviors? Let's have a look at what these numbers mean in relation to some of the marketing strategies ole' Chip offers.

## Marketing Numbers Don't Lie!

- At the time of this writing insiderpages.com gets 5 million visitors per month... *and counting.*
- Superpages.com gets 35 Million visitors per month... *and counting.*
- The review site "Yelp" gets 78 Million unique visitors per month... *and counting.*
- Facebook, 955 million monthly active users at the end of June 2012, visitors per month... *and counting.*
- Google gets 1 Billion visitors per month... *and counting.*

**All of these numbers are expected to rise over the next few years.**
**And in case that's not hitting close enough to home...**

Reviews Impact the New Connections and Sales from all your web properties including: your website, PPC landing pages, Yelp page, Google +local profile page, Yahoo page, YP.com page, Kudzoo page, Citysearch page, Mojopages profile page, Judy's Book profile page etc.

Would you bet on the claims and promises of "Chip the Cheat" or on the numbers gathered by observing human buying behaviors? Let's have a look at what these numbers mean in relation to some of the marketing strategies ole' Chip offers.

## The Marriage of Pay Per Click and Reviews

Would you pay $1 for just a few seconds of someone's attention? It sounds absurd, I know, but that's what you'll end up doing if your PPC ads aren't supported by positive reviews. If you spend any money on PPC advertising, you already know how important it is for someone to click on your ad.

But you also know those clicks can add up really fast if you're not getting conversions. If you're investing money into PPC and having failing results, it's like having Google hook a vacuum cleaner up to your account and suck all the money out. It's scary, and it can make you never want to touch PPC marketing again. This is why reviews are vital not just for SEO, but for PPC as well.

It used to be that if you had problems with SEO you could circumvent the organic listings by just paying for sponsored listings. But yet again, Google wants their users to have the best results possible and will reward you for having a high click-through-rate. This means you can outbid a competitor for clicks, but if your ad "quality score" is low, your competitor will STILL get better search positioning than you even if you pay more. On top of this, ratings and reviews are now appearing in sponsored listings too! What could affect the power of a PPC listing more than dozens or hundreds of five-star ratings?

Again, a PPC ad which has a lot of clicks will achieve a higher "quality score" and be pushed to the top of the search results page on Google, even if the advertiser isn't the highest bidder. Illustrated in the graphic below, ratings and references to reviews are now being posted directly beside PPC ads, thus having a direct effect on the click-through-rate of PPC ads.

Your Local **Plumbers** - $33 Off. Is Today Soon Enough?
maps.google.com/FurnaceRepair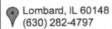
Check Out Our Great **Reviews**!

⚲ Lombard, IL 60148
♀ (630) 282-4797

★★★★★
59 reviews

Ads related to heating                                      Why these ads?

Brea **Heating** - **Heating** Company for 50+ Years.
www.plumbing-htg-ac-ca.com/
Call 714-784-5578 for Prompt Service!

Put yourself in the consumer's shoes. Which of the ads would you be more likely to click on? The one which has 59 reviews and an average of 4.5 stars, or the ad which isn't showing any ratings or reviews? Of course, having no reviews at all will soon become a non-issue because every service company will have online ratings and links to reviews in the search results next to their ads. The question is whether the service company will be proactively involved in earning positive reviews from their customers.

If someone clicks on the reviews link in your PPC ads and sees scores of mediocre or poor reviews about your company, how likely do you think they are to even click through and visit your website? If they do click on your site, how fast do you think they'll click away from your web pages if it doesn't show them enough up-to-date positive reviews? Probably just a few seconds, and if you're paying even $1 per click, you've just paid a dollar for a few seconds of someone's attention. This combination of a poor click-through-rate with a high bounce rate means either a lower position, or more money paid just to keep your ad in front of people. So don't let "The Pied Pipers of Pay Per Click" fool you, if you're not highly recommended, PPC is very likely just a waste of money.

## The Company That Rocks the Reviews is the Company that Rules the Market

If someone's searching for your company name or the kind of service you offer, you can be ninety-nine percent sure they're already sold on the service you provide. Would you turn away someone who was in need of your services and let them go to your competitors instead? Yes, your service might be better than your competitors, but your potential customer doesn't know that. To them, you might as well be offering the *same thing* as your competitor. Where does that leave you when it comes to closing the deal and earning their business? You're reduced to competing on price or trying to spend more on advertising. After all, why should your customer do business with you when in their mind they can get the same thing for less money somewhere else?

Even if your service is better, your prospective customer won't see that unless your *existing customers* give them a reason to check you out.

This is where a lot of businesses are forced to settle for the "best price" marketing angle. They don't have anything else to go on. Let's face it if you're in the service business, selling services isn't that hard. You find a customer who has the problem your service solves, you demonstrate that you understand them, you tell them how your service can solve their problem, you close the deal and you go away. The problem is, your customer isn't asking, "Why should I order *this service*?" That's already a done deal. The question they're asking is, "Why should I order this service from *your company* instead of that company?

Can you provide them a believable reason for choosing you? Ask most business owners this and they'll come back with a generic answer like: "We provide great services," or, "We're the best deal in town," or, "We provide a 100 percent money back guarantee." Not only is that a lot of "we-we" marketing, but won't your competitors say the same things about themselves? It's pretty much your word against theirs. Again, you're reduced to selling based on price alone or trying to rule your competition by spending more money on advertising. But even this won't make a bit of difference if your competitor has you buried when it comes to positive customer reviews.

Are you starting to see how being remarkable is the secret to sales and company growth? So what are you going to do about it? If you're up for the challenge, and you're sick of depending on marketing theories, let me tell you about a company that turned reviews into sales power.

## How Tempur-Pedic Turned Remark-ability into Marketing Ability

The graphic below is an example of the Tempur-Pedic "Ask me" campaign.

Imagine seeing this advertisement next to a $10,000 piece of "we-we" marketing created by an award-winning marketing firm. I know, the "we-we" marketing would give you more fancy designs to ooh and ahh over, but Tempur-

Pedic wasn't out to win marketing awards, they were out to win customers.

They used the "Ask Me" campaign to *proactively* turn authentic customer reviews into marketing campaigns and commercials. Before they started this campaign, Tempur-pedic's sales were down by over 30 percent. It was the beginning of the recession in 2009, but Tempur-pedic decided to invest when everyone else was pulling back. What really mattered was what they invested in and how it led to a 70 percent increase in sales during the first half of 2010. (*Source: Social Network Feedback Sparks Tempur-Pedic's Sales*, Investors.com, Feb. 4, 2011)

Tempur-Pedic's Secret Weapon was to put their customers first so they would become more than Ravers. The customers *became* the face of the company, saying exactly what Tempur-Pedic wanted their *new* customers to hear.

Do you think this strategic word-of-mouth marketing would have been possible without offering remarkable customer service and a great product? Do you think those advertisements would have been as effective if they'd simply been endorsements by a Tempur-Pedic sales person, celebrity, or actress/actor? It almost doesn't matter what product you're selling, customer opinion is the undisputed champion of sales, of marketing and of company growth. Anyone who says differently is probably "we-we" marketing their own "award winning" marketing services.

# Imagine: More Money per Sale

I don't have any Google screen shots to show you on this one because neither companies nor customers are going to share information about how much is being spent. Instead, I want to remind you of Chris's experience in making more money per sale because he conquered the trust barrier. When that happens, you're perceived more like a friend and a guest in the person's home rather than a target of suspicion and skepticism.

Most companies can't focus on creating value and selling additional services because they're too busy spinning their wheels trying to keep up with getting new prospects and turning those prospects into sales. Some of these companies are running just to keep up. Meanwhile, you can cut through the drama of overcoming objections by having a high level of trust from the beginning. This way your sales people and technicians can build relationships, offer value and sell more services.

# Imagine: More Referrals

Any good book or article you read on sales and marketing will tell you that you have to ask for referrals. Having positive online reviews puts your referral process on autopilot. A single online review can affect the buying decisions of dozens, hundreds or even thousands of customers, and for years and years after the review was even written.

Having postitive
online reviews
puts your
referral process
on **autopilot.**

Having online reviews eliminates the need for your customers to do something that most consumers don't like to do: try and sell their friends and family members on your company. By writing an online review, a customer can refer hundreds of people to your company with just a click of a mouse.

Those reviews work for you tirelessly, day and night, even while the customers who wrote them are sound asleep.

Remember, we're not just talking about online marketing. Imagine having a salesperson or a service person come to your door, not alone, but accompanied by dozens of past customers in the form of online reviews that you can read instantly from their notebook or iPad. In essence, they arrive with letters of recommendations in the form of raving customer reviews about themselves and their company. You can't beat that with a sledgehammer, my friend. But it all starts, not with making sales, but with creating remarkable experiences for your customers.

## Lessons from Scarface's Tony Montana

In the epic mobster flick, *Scarface*, there was a scene when Manny was trying to get the attention of the women at the resort and ended up getting smacked for an indecent gesture. That's when the main character, Tony, laughs and tells Manny, "Listen. In this country you gotta make the money first. Then when you get the money, you get the power. Then when you get the power, then you get the women." So his formula looks like this:

1. Earn the Money
2. Get the Power
3. Get the Women

Well this is my version: "Listen. In today's customer-driven digital age, before you can get a sale you gotta earn the review, once you get the review, you get the Review Power and then you get the sale."

But before you get the Review Power, you have to be remark-*able* Therefore, my formula looks like this:

1. *Earn* the Review
2. Get the Review
3. Get the Sale

Again, the golden goose (remark-*ability*) is your most valuable asset, not your money and not even your reviews and it begins and ends with delivering exceptional service.

# Chapter Four Summary:

1. If you master new connections, new sales and maximize your per sale average and get customer referrals, you're firing on all cylinders when it comes to marketing. Most companies dump a ton of money into those four things, yet a single solution can solve all four of them.

2. When you have dozens or even hundreds of customers saying you're the best, you get to skip the skepticism and objections that come with a new client relationship and cut right to the process of adding value.

3. More customers buy because of online reviews than any other form of advertising.

4. Being Remark-*able* is the hidden-in-plain-sight-but-hard-to-face secret of sales and company growth.

5. If you're not being remarkable, PPC is just a waste of money.

6. It almost doesn't matter what product you're selling, customer opinion is the undisputed champion of sales, marketing and company growth.

7. Having positive online reviews puts your referral process on autopilot.

# Chapter 4 Recommended Reading

*Good to Great: Why Some Companies Make the Leap...
and Others Don't*, Jim Collins (HarperBusiness, 2001)

# Chapter 5

# Rule 4: Beware the "Fool's Gold"

By now you realize that digital word-of-mouth marketing is the most important item on your to-do list to growing a profitable business.

But before you get too excited and start working on ways to use this powerful tool on your own I want to make sure you're not heading down the wrong path — one that could get you banned from Google and other highly critical review sites. Yes, that's right, Google can put an Internet smack down on you so fast you'll think your server short circuited.

To illustrate the difference between doing this right and plummeting down the black hole of Google's black list, let me tell you the parable of two competing service companies. Both companies worked hard to earn the respect of their customers, but they each chose a different path for their review management practices.

Once upon a time, there were two service companies: Joe's company, "Junior Achiever, Inc." and Lou's company, "Super-Goose, Inc."

Junior Achiever called up a review syndication service to help them punch up their online reputation by posting some positive reviews on various review sites like Google+, Yahoo Local, and Yelp.

The marketing manager for Junior Achiever supplied the review syndication company with a stack of comment cards, all with real testimonials written by Junior Achiever's happy customers. These comment cards were re-purposed into online reviews by a review syndication company that created fake accounts on review sites so the *real* comments from the comment cards could be seen by everyone online.

The review syndication service was also calling Junior Achiever's current customers after each job, asking them about their experience and getting testimonials to post online "on the customer's behalf."

Seems like a good idea so far, right? Keep reading...

Super-Goose decided to take another path. They chose to create such a remark-*able* experience that their customer was motivated to post online reviews using their own accounts on sites such as Google+ Local, Yahoo Local, Yelp, and Facebook.

Super-Goose's efforts resulted in a legitimate social network. For instance, their Facebook page had a strong following of *real* fans and the benefit was every friend and family member connected to those fans saw their positive review. This has the potential to expand Super-Goose's visibility exponentially. In addition, when a review was posted on Google+ Local, or Yelp, Super-Goose promptly shared that review on Facebook and Twitter to help spread the buzz even further.

In contrast, although Junior Achiever had some nice reviews, they were on fabricated review accounts and fake social network accounts. They weren't connected to the social web in any way. These fake reviewers did not have hundreds of friends or family members linking to them. Instead it was as if the reviews were produced by an invisible person with no connection to other real people. There was no further visibility for Junior Achiever beyond the initial review.

Junior Achiever soon realized that these reviews carried very little weight and they might have put their digital foot in their mouth by posting *for* their customers instead of motivating their customers to post their own reviews.

Meanwhile Super-Goose had reviews written by *real* customers on their *real* personal accounts and seen by a circle of *real* friends. As a result, their phone was ringing off the hook with digital word-of-mouth referrals! They were reaping the rewards of creating virtual marketing.

Fast forward one year later.

Junior Achiever felt trapped. They had spent the last twelve months having virtually invisible reviews posted but they knew if they stopped paying the syndication service they would simultaneously stop getting reviews. They treated getting reviews as the end all to growing their business, when what they didn't realize was the review was the reward for providing remark-*able* service. Their focus was misdirected and they were going to pay the price for this mistake.

On the other hand, Super-Goose spent the past year feeding their golden goose by working out a streamlined system for getting their customers to post real reviews on highly influential sites. Now they had hundreds and hundreds of positive reviews being seen by not only their online fans and prospects, but all of the friends of those fans.

You might think Junior Achievement had nothing to fear because they also had a lot of reviews that were created by their review syndication service — right? Then one day something strange happened... Junior Achiever logged on to Yahoo Local to check on their reviews and they were all gone! In addition their website was no longer showing up on Google! Yes, that's right they got the smack down and were KO'd online.

To make matters worse, not only is Junior Achiever a year behind Super-Goose in getting legitimate customer reviews and real social buzz, but their incoming phone calls have dropped by 80 percent.

What happened?! I'll tell you what happened: "Open mouth, insert foot."

Junior Achiever didn't do their homework and make sure the practices being used by their review syndication company were acceptable to Google, Yahoo and other review sites. They thought getting customers to post reviews was difficult or even impossible so they took the shortcut. They fell for fool's gold.

Junior Achiever had their Yahoo reviews deleted because they weren't created by real Yahoo users. They were banned from Google for breaking the rules and not following Google's terms of use.

"Advertising and spam: Don't use reviews for advertising or post the same or similar reviews across multiple places, and don't post fake reviews intended to boost or lower ratings."

*(Source: Google Places Policies and Guidelines)*

**Disclaimer:** Google reserves the right to suspend access to Google Places or other Google Services to individuals or businesses that violate these guidelines, and may work with law enforcement in the event that the violation is unlawful.

(Source: Google Places Policies and Guidelines)

Junior Achiever now has three chances of catching up with Super-Goose: Fat, Slim, or None. In fact we all know what happens if Google suddenly turned off the switch. You know the outcome of this story — enough said.

This may seem like a fairytale, but it is a grim reality that has befallen service companies that give into temptation and take the shortcut.

There's a saying that goes: "Not all that glitters is gold." This is especially true with regard to using reviews to grow your business.

## Google and the Golden Rule against Fool's Gold

We all know the golden rule...

*"So in everything, do unto others what you would have them do to you."*

Few of us realize that the golden rule is Google's primary defense against fool's gold. Google is continuously refining their technology to make sure the golden rule dictates the Google search results.

As far as consumers and Internet users are concerned, genuine User Generated Content (UGC) such as customer reviews, testimonials and even complaints about a company are more credible than company-generated advertisements.

That's what people want, and that's what Google is determined to deliver.

Google wants to give users exactly what any reasonable person would want: the truth about a company, their products and their services. Google is in the trust business, and the more trust they earn from Internet users by providing better search results, the more valuable Google becomes.

"We want people to get ratings, reviews, and recommendations that are relevant, helpful and trustworthy."

(Source: Google Places, Policy and Guidelines)

"Being bad is, and hopefully will always be, bad for business in Google's search results,"

Amit Singal
Google Software Engineer
(Source: New Google Algorithm To Punish Bad Businesses, Xtmotion.co.uk Dec. 8, 2011)

It's extremely important that you become aware of any policies enforced by Google that could pertain to your business practices, especially your content. For most service companies today Google is the foremost food supply for your goose in the form of leads, phone calls, and customers.

To understand *why* Google develops the policies and systems they put in place, you have to understand their motivations. Google's goose is fed by having consumers use their site, and then being able to charge businesses to advertise to those consumers.

Just as it's important for your company to be remarkable to keep customers coming back and recommending you to others, it's also extremely important for Google to provide *remarkable search results* so online shoppers keep coming back and referring other shoppers. If Google wants to stay on top, they have to make sure the search results they provide have extreme value for their users.

For example, a shopper goes to Google to find a tanning salon. Google wants to make sure they not only find tanning salons close by but they help the shopper find the *BEST* tanning salon for their needs and preferences.

If Google operated like the Yellow Pages book, the shopper's experience would be much different. With the Yellow Pages, the search experience is hit or miss. There is very limited information from which to make an educated decision and the shopper could have a terrible experience. When it's time to choose again, the shopper uses Yelp instead and is able to get social proof about each of the listings by reading reviews and checking out customer star ratings.

That's why Google has implemented policies and systems that *reward* companies that provide remarkable service by following the Golden Rule, and *penalize* companies that don't.

(Source: Google Places Policies and Guidelines)

## Syndicated vs. Impersonated: What's the difference?

So by now you know the fool's gold of reputation management is review impersonation. But it's very important to understand that in Google's eyes, and in the eyes of the consumers and review sites, there's no difference between review syndication and impersonation. Reviews are basically guilty until proven innocent…and the proof is in the users account. Calling it "review syndication," doesn't change that either, you're just spray-painting the goose's eggs gold.

That reminds me of a riddle Abe Lincoln used to tell:

*"If you call a dog's tail a leg, how many legs does it have?"*

The answer isn't five, it's four. Calling a tail a leg doesn't make it a leg. It's the same with review impersonation. You can call it syndication all you want, but Google has the final word so let's see what they say:

> **"Impersonation: Don't post reviews on behalf of others or misrepresent your identity or affiliation with the place you are reviewing. We don't allow impersonation or behavior that is misleading or intended to be misleading."**
>
> *(Source: Google Places Policies and Guidelines)*

The practice of review syndication used by some companies involves going out on the web and creating reviews on behalf of a company for the purpose of making them *appear* trustworthy.

These "reviews" are either written by someone working for the review management company or they are gathered from testimonials written on customer comment cards. In many cases, the same review is re-purposed under different names and posted on multiple review sites. All these are examples of review impersonation. So to show you just how easy it is to fall for fool's gold, let's look at a few common practices of review syndication companies. See if you can spot which of these are authentic review practices:

1. Create fake accounts on multiple review sites.
2. Use proxies and multiple IP addresses (technical terms - more on this shortly) to make it look like many users in multiple locations are posting the reviews.
3. Hire professional writers to fabricate reviews.
4. Syndicate these so-called "reviews" across multiple review sites.
5. Recycle reviews for several other customers who own businesses like yours.
6. Call their clients' customers after the job and ask them for testimonials and get their permission to post those testimonials online.

The answer is: none of them. Even number six is off limits because there's no way for the public to verify whether the reviews are real. This might not seem fair if you've earned hundreds of customer testimonials which are posted on comment cards or written to you via emails. Save those for your website or marketing collateral. The reality is that reviews are guilty until proven innocent and the review sites have the final say on what's authentic and what's not.

Again, call this what you want; syndication, authentication, makin' way for the great celebration of the

Golden Goose sensation. Take the fancy words away and it's all the same thing: impersonation.

If you want to protect the credibility and reputation of your company and your industry and avoid being sent down the wrong path by shady reputation management companies or SEO experts, then you need to know what's really going on out there.

You owe it to yourself, your employees and to the unsuspecting consumers to become educated about these false practices.

## Who's Watching You?

Do you remember this expression? "The definition of character is what you do when you think no one is looking." When it comes to manufacturing reviews, you might be surprised at how many people are watching you.

## The Feds Will Hurt Your Wallet

The FTC (Federal Trade Commission) has fined companies as much as $250,000 for using services that write fake reviews. They considered fake reviews to fall under the rules of deceptive business practices and false advertising. (Source: *Firm to Pay FTC $250, 000 to Settle Charges That It Used Misleading Online "Consumer" and "Independent" Reviews*, FTC.gov, March 15, 2011)

Check your bank account. Do you have a quarter million dollars sitting around and absolutely nothing useful to spend it on? Can you imagine having that debt hanging over your head just because you took the easy way out or you trusted a company who told you, "don't worry, we do this all the time" when it comes creating reviews on your behalf?

## The Bloggers Write in Ink

*Company name blacked out to protect identity.

One service company that hired a so-called "syndication" service had their online reputation destroyed and they had to pay tens of thousands of dollars just to have a Public Relations firm help them clean up the mess. The company spent the next few months defending themselves via a blog thread before ultimately abandoning the review syndication service. Of course, even after they stopped using the service, that blog thread remained, with their company name painted all over it.

Funny thing about blogs, they're not like newspapers. People don't just read them and throw them away. Blog readers comment on the posts, follow one another's comments, and interact with each other. Those blog posts and the responses are then picked up by the search engines.

The term "written in stone" is quickly becoming replaced with the term "written in blog," so keep that in mind when you're building your online reputation. All it takes is for *one* frustrated blogger to discover a fake review about your company and your reputation carries that negative blog post forever (literally and virtually). If it shows up in search results (which it very likely could if people start linking to it) it will be as attractive to your customers as a roach on a birthday cake. Imagine the impact of a blog written about you that

**"The Internet is not written in pencil. It's written in ink."**

*(Source: The Social Network Movie, Relativity Media, 2010)*

provides proof that you used less-than-authentic means for earning reviews. It would be like having the word "Cheater" permanently tattooed across your forehead. Blog reviews give a new meaning to the expression, "the writing's on the wall." Consumers don't want to take the risk of spending money with a company other people have deemed dishonest or unprofessional.

## The Whistle Blowing Consumers Unite

Do you want to make people mad enough to get them talking about your company? Mess with their money; it's a sure way to get the job done. As I mentioned before, consumers are more well-informed today than ever before. They'll Google you, Facebook you, look you up on YouTube and LinkedIn, and you can't stop them.

If they find out you're saying false things or using unethical advertising practices in an attempt to get them to hand their money over, you might as well be trying to hack into their bank account. They're going to talk. They'll tell their Facebook friends, their Twitter followers and all their Google+ circles. They'll point fingers and name names.

They'll even trash you on popular consumer watchdog forums like RipoffReport.com; sites that have enough public influence to take you down faster than Chris Hanson from Dateline NBC. Even if the report isn't one hundred percent true, you can't just have a comment removed from RipoffReport.com. Ever.

In fact, in preparation for writing this book, I paid to have people research this option and I assure you it's nearly impossible to have a bad report removed without spending tens of thousands of dollars, and even that is not guaranteed. To make matters worse *the site consistently ranks on Page One when you Google any company mentioned in one of their reports!* The venting of a disgruntled whistle blower will be forever etched into the tablet of cyberspace. Trying to get your name off the bad boy list is like putting a Band-Aid on a hemorrhaging artery. Remember, the bad review is not the issue; the reason for the bad review IS the issue.

I've also seen these types of "fake review outing" posts spark responses from other readers which turns into entire discussions fueled by an army of pissed-off consumers, most of them have never even heard of you before but who are united by their outrage against consumer injustice. They pour their words out into cyberspace like a steady flow of B.S. repellent. At best you can hire a super charismatic PR person to join the discussion, but I bet even Bill Clinton couldn't talk his way out of this one.

And if that's not enough…

# The Robots Are On Autopilot

Considering how valuable the credibility of online reviews is to consumer sites like Google and Yelp, it's no surprise that teams of some of the sharpest minds are working feverishly to crack the code of fake and impersonated reviews. It won't be long before search engines and review sites are sporting the latest B.S.-detector technologies in the pursuit of identifying manipulative and deceptive review-generation practices. In fact, a team of researchers at Cornell University claim to have developed software algorithms that are able to detect fake reviews at a *ninety percent* accuracy rate!

# Cornell software fingers fake online reviews

 by Eric Smalley | July 26, 2011 10:36 AM PDT

If you're like most people, you give yourself high ratings when it comes to figuring out when someone's trying to con you. Problem is, most people aren't *actually* good at it--at least as far as detecting fake positive consumer reviews.

Fortunately, technology is poised to make up for this all-too-human failing. Cornell University researchers have developed software that they say can detect fake reviews (PDF). The researchers tested the system with reviews of Chicago hotels. They pooled 400 truthful reviews with 400 deceptive reviews produced for the study, then trained their software to spot the difference.

The software got it right about 90 percent of the time. This is a big improvement over the average person, who can detect fake reviews only about 50 percent of the time, according to the researchers.

(Source: *Cornell Software Fingers Fake Online Reviews*, CNET, 26 July 2011)

Their findings were presented in a July 22, 2011 report from Cornell University entitled, *Finding Deceptive Opinion Spam by Any Stretch of the Imagination*. I won't post the entire eleven-page report — it's chock full of scientific jargon — but here's the summary of their findings (underline emphasis is mine):

*Conclusion and Future Work*

*"In this work we have developed the first large-scale dataset containing gold-standard deceptive opinion spam.*

*With it, we have shown that the detection of deceptive opinion spam is well beyond the capabilities of human judges, most of whom perform roughly at-chance. Accordingly, <u>we have introduced three automated approaches to deceptive opinion spam detection, based on insights coming from research in computational linguistics and psychology.</u>"*

You might have noticed the term "deceptive opinion spam" used above. "Deceptive opinion spam" is not the same thing as review syndication, but it can get you into trouble just as fast. In the report above, deceptive opinion spam refers to outright fake reviews being written and posted on review site accounts or reviews made up by friends and family members of the company in question.

While review syndication practices might not fall squarely under the category of "deception," the practices are definitely and expressly prohibited by Google and Yelp and the other review sites. Remember, all reviews are guilty until proven innocent by Google standards, or the standards of the review site. Just like deceptive reviews can be detected by computer software, so too can impersonated reviews be detected.

For example, all online activity can be traced to a time and a place and even a particular computer, narrowing the options for businesses to game the system and fake their way into high rankings. Earlier in this chapter, I mentioned IP addresses. To put this into perspective, the IP address is like the unique "fingerprint" which your computer uses to connect with the network of computers we know as the internet. The moment you connect to the internet, your IP becomes visible to anyone who has the technology to track it, and just to show you how easy that is to do, here's the block of programming code that reveals the IP address of ANY computer that visits your website:

```php
<?php

$ip = @$REMOTE_ADDR;

?>
```

With only a couple more lines of code we could narrow that IP address down to a specific geographical location, complete with a Google Maps satellite reference that shows a picture of the user's exact location. Now do you believe Google can tell when someone writes a bunch of reviews from the same IP address? Any reasonably experienced programmer can write another page of code and create an automated program that tracks the "behaviors" coming from each IP address and flags them for anything suspicious. If enough violations come up, Google will take action to punish the benefiting party.

A good indicator of a questionable review syndication company is to ask them about this IP address issue. What you will probably hear is some version of this response: "Oh, but we use multiple IP addresses so we won't be detected,"

If you hear this, you can bet an avalanche of B.S. is coming next. At least you'll know for sure that they are willfully violating the rules of online review management and using multiple IP addresses won't cover the trail. It will simply give Google more records to add to their blacklist, and sooner or later, those IP trails will lead back to a fake account with a fake review. If one of those reviews has YOUR company's name on it…game over.

On top of all this, it's only a matter of time before artificial intelligence software is able to detect both fake reviews and impersonated reviews with nearly one hundred percent accuracy. When that day comes, all those fake and impersonated reviews — the ones that have been bought by service companies that chose the shortcut — will disappear in the blink of an eye.

If you're one of those companies you'll be *lucky* if you don't get banned from Google altogether. Speaking of Google, let's wrap this up by seeing what they have to say about the new rules of online review management.

## Google is Investing

I'm not the only one who believes in the future of online reviews. Some pretty intelligent people over there at Google seem to find the credibility of their reviews to be important enough to have offered to purchase Yelp for a reported *$500 million*. Although their offer was rejected, they didn't give up easily. (My hunch is the reason they wanted Yelp so badly has something to do with Yelp's trademark tagline, "Real People. Real Reviews.")

Now if that's not convincing enough, Google recently purchased online survey company, Zagat in a deal worth $151 million! Is Google just in the habit of collecting review sites at $100 million + a pop? Probably not, I'm guessing that they know something about the power and the influence of real reviews. Just check out what Google had to say about why they think Zagat is a good investment that will improve their search result efforts (again, underlined emphasis is mine):

*"[Zagat's] surveys may be one of the earliest forms of UGC (user-generated content) - gathering restaurant recommendations from friends, computing and distributing ratings before the Internet as we know it today even existed," wrote Marissa Mayer, Google's Vice President of Local, Maps and Location Services, when the deal was announced. "Their iconic pocket-sized guides with paragraphs summarizing and "snippeting" sentiment were "mobile" before "mobile" involved electronics. Today, Zagat provides people with a democratized, authentic and*

*comprehensive view of where to eat, drink, stay, shop and play worldwide <u>based on millions of reviews and ratings.</u>"*

*"<u>Our goal in making changes to the way we present search results is to get people the information they're looking for as quickly and effortlessly as possible</u>," a Google spokeswoman said in an email.*

Zagat announced the acquisition on its website and once Google changed the review process their star rating system was replaced with the well-known Zagat Score in which 30 out of 30 was the coveted prize all businesses strived to attain. "Zagat, a 'pioneer in user-generated content' and creator of the world's most 'influential' and 'trusted' consumer reviews, has been acquired by another 'renowned innovator,' GOOGLE," the *review* read. The review of "Google" gave the company a top score of 30 on "local," "social," "mobile" and "useful," categories that usually read "food," "decor," "service" and "cost" in Zagat's restaurant reviews. (Source: *Google Adds More Of Its Own Goodies To Search Results, Despite Antitrust Concerns*, The Huffington Post, Nov 2, 2011)

What we're talking about here, again, is location. There's a reason Google was willing to pay so much money for this review site rather than buy up the dozens of low-value, low-visibility sites. Google understands this principle, and that's why they're dominating the Internet.

Google is so determined to set a standard of intolerance that I've seen companies who no longer rank on Page One for *their own company name!* Can you imagine what that could mean for someone who had heard of you — even heard positive things — and who decided to Google your company name? They type your company name in and your site is nowhere to be found. Instead, your search results are loaded with links to other sites where people are talking about your company and saying unfavorable things.

It's not just Google's probing bots (spider robots that search the Internet looking for duplicate, relevant or irrelevant content) that you have to worry about. Contrary to common assumptions, Google does use *real human beings* to manually review websites and spot fraud. While I was interviewing potential contractors for my Internet marketing company, I met with a young lady who was subcontracted by Google to check out websites, review sites, and social media sites to report back to Google any suspicious activity such as fake reviews.

It can get really, really ugly my friend. If this happens to you it's like the old saying goes, *"Your goose is cooked!"* and a cooked goose can't lay any more golden eggs.

## Other Business Owners Have Eyes

If you've thought about making an end-run around creating positive reviews for your own company by trashing your competition, you'll want to think again. Business owners just like you are keeping a close eye on the source of the positive and negative reviews they receive. Just as they are seeking to thank those people who have taken the time to write glowing reviews, they are spending even more time making sure the negative ones are legitimate.

Just recently a disgruntled former business partner posted three fake derogatory reviews about his ex-partner's business using the names of prior customers on Yahoo and Google. Not only did the partner take the steps to require Yahoo and Google to identify the author of the reviews, he filed a defamation suit against his former partner. The court found in favor of the defamed partner and ordered the originator of the fake reviews to pay $150,000 in punitive damages. Remember, nothing is truly anonymous on the internet! (Source: Missouri Court of Appeals – Court Transcript – Digital Commons.law.scu.edu)

Google has taken this issue of fake reviews even further. In the past you were able to use any Gmail account to log in and write a review. Now you must have a legitimate Google+ account, which requires you to use your real name, not a made up username, to write content. This move brings more validity to the review process than ever before. With a price tag of $150,000, is trying to game the system worth it?

## If Your Goose is Laying Rotten Eggs, You Can't Just Paint Them Gold

Besides the rare disgruntled ex-partner fake reviews, if you're attracting bad reviews about your company, this means your goose is laying *rotten* eggs. As I mentioned previously, spray-painting those eggs gold won't change anything.

Even if you're not planning to break any laws or post fake reviews, if you have to hire a reputation management company to fix your online reputation, you're not addressing the real issue. The real issue is how you're serving your customers.

If I haven't stressed it enough, getting positive reviews is critical to your success, but that's not the core focus of this book. The focus is to inspire and execute a plan to create a customer experience and a company culture which *naturally lends itself to the accumulation of positive, authentic reviews.* It's about training your goose to lay those golden eggs and how to cash in on them once they arrive. Transparent communication and engagement is not a fad.

The bottom line is this, things are changing quickly and following trends won't make you wildly successful online because there's too much competition. You have to start by understanding the consumer behaviors that create trends that force the search engines and social media sites to change their business model. Google and the other search engines are applying quality control principles to every piece of content on the Internet, and the content which doesn't make the grade will be buried in the virtual graveyard of spam sites and link farms.

So before you consider hiring a reputation management company, let me give you a few easy "Dos and Don'ts" that will keep you out of trouble and put you on the right path toward gathering up your review power so that you can dominate your competition in the new world of online marketing.

## The 3 Don'ts of Earning Reviews

First let's start with what *not* to do. As I told you earlier there are some practices which are frowned upon by Google. In fact they are so abhorrent to Google that they will eject you from the ring if they catch you fighting dirty.

1. DON'T post fake reviews which includes posting reviews using fake accounts.
2. DON'T impersonate your customers. Remember Google's rules. Customer testimonials cannot be turned into reviews by creating a fake account with a review site on the customer's behalf
3. DON'T offer incentives for reviews — Google calls it a "conflict of interest" but let's call it what it really is — bribery. Don't offer your customers money, favors, merchandise, free service, or anything else of value in exchange for posting reviews online

## The 3 Dos of Earning Reviews

It's not fair to drop some "Thou shalt nots" in your lap and leave you to figure out a code of review morality that works, so let's talk about a few things that you *can* do to increase your social capital without risking the farm.

1.  DO turn your happy customers into promoters — With very little money and effort you can create a system that will turn your happy customers into marketing machines that will go out into the world and market your business for you. The next two "Dos" will help you make this happen.

2.  DO train your team to *earn, win* and *request* online reviews. When you know you've created a remarkable experience and built a bond with your customer, asking for the review is easy. As your staff becomes more engaged in providing these remarkable experiences they'll become more comfortable asking for reviews.

3.  DO make it easy for your customers to post reviews — You may think it's simple to post a review, but to some people it's much the same as learning how to solve a Rubik's Cube. Make it as easy as possible for them. First, give them a direct link to your review pages so they don't have to go looking for them. Second, give them clear and simple step-by-step instructions on how to post a review. Customers are often wary of creating a new account on a review site, so give them a few options.

So there you have it, three critical steps *not* to take, and three essential steps *to* take if you want to be favored in the eyes of the gatekeepers of social capital and not be banned from the kingdom of Google. Follow these rules and you'll do just fine.

"Okay, enough already! How do I start making this work Mike?"

I hope you're asking this, because you're about to catch a wave of success that your competitors don't even see coming. It all depends on whether or not you're ready for my answer, which is *"If you want more golden eggs, ya gotta start with the goose."*

Forget all about getting reviews for a minute and pay really close attention because the rubbers about to meet the road.

# Chapter Five Summary:

1.  Be aware, and wary of review syndication services to make sure they are following all the acceptable terms of use of Google, Yelp, and other trusted and influential review sites.

2.  Everyone is watching you from the Federal government, to Google robots, bloggers, and whistle-blower consumers. Less-than-authentic reviews will be found and your business may risk being blackballed online.

3.  If you have to hire a reputation management company to fix your online reputation, you're not addressing the real issue.

4.  Transparent communication and engagement is not a fad.

5.  Follow the 3 Do's and Don'ts of gaining review power.

# Chapter 5 Recommended Reading

*The SPEED of Trust: The One Thing That Changes Everything*, Stephen M.R. Covey (Free Press, 2008)

# Chapter 6

# Rule 5: Build a Buzz-Winning Team

You've probably been aching for me to unload the turn-key secret to winning reviews so you could close this book and get on with applying what you've learned.

To become remarkable, you have to make being exceptional an operational focus and building your remarkable team, one person at a time. This is how some of the most successful companies of the past decade got where they are right now. You've been introduced to some of them in this book:

- Zappos
- Apple
- Nordstrom
- Google
- *Your company?*

Whether or not your company belongs on this list will depend on how you apply the final rule of becoming remarkable: building a great team and buzz-winning company culture.

Turning remark-*ability* into marketing *ability* isn't just about earning and posting great reviews, it starts with being remark-*able*. As service companies all over the country start realizing the power of online reviews, a lot of them will end up in a *"Which came first the goose or the golden egg?"* dilemma. They'll start getting aggressive about the golden eggs — the reviews — instead of getting obsessed with feeding the goose through remarkable customer experiences. But only those who start with the goose will strike gold.

# What is a Buzz Winning Culture?

I realize the word "culture" is thrown around a lot these days. Some of us think culture is something you get from traveling to a foreign country or spending your weekends at tea parties and sushi bars listening to chamber music.

I thought I'd make this really simple by using a definition I plucked out of the Merriam-Webster Dictionary:

Culture: *"The set of shared attitudes, values, goals and practices that characterizes an institution or organization."*

If I were to ask you what attitudes, values, goals and practices characterize your organization, what would you say? Better yet, if I were to ask your *employees,* what would they say? How about if I were to ask your *customers?* That's the real test isn't it?

It's easy to say you're "cultivating an extraordinary, customer-focused culture," and then reprint it on a poster with your company logo and put it just above the coffee maker in your break room. But that's just "we-we" marketing, and it won't persuade your employees any more than it will persuade your customers. If you want to become remarkable, you have to start by facing the hard facts about what changes need to be made to your company's operational systems and the way you manage what is measurable.

You've probably worked for at least one company who insisted that they valued a remarkable customer experience but who didn't support that claim in their training, team meetings, rewards, incentives or communications. It was just a theory, a story the company leaders told each other while sitting around in stuffy corporate meetings. These companies remain stuck, not because they can't fix their company culture, but because they've convinced themselves that their culture doesn't need to be reexamined.

This is exactly where we don't want to be. That's why our final rule will focus on the five key elements of building a remarkable company culture:

1. Smart Hiring
2. Training
3. Accountability
4. Recognition
5. Leadership

Get these elements right and I promise you everything in this book will take care of itself: the reviews, the Google rankings, the sales, the growth, the conquering of your competition, the Olympic caliber golden-egg-laying goose...all of it.

## Hiring Remarkable People: Who Has the Golden Goose DNA?

Customer service is one of those things you either have in your DNA or you don't. I'm not saying customer service can't be taught. Heck, I've seen some borderline wallflowers converted into full-blown customer service powerhouses with the right training. But it's important to know how to hire people who have the *potential* for remark-*ability* in their blood. It's not for everyone. There are people who just don't like people, don't like serving others and who would rather sit behind a computer, crunch numbers and judge everyone else who is different from them. Occasionally, some of these people try to venture into the world of customer service. Sometimes they put on a very good show and get you to hire them. Once you start working with them you get the feeling you're trying to teach a horse how to climb a tree.

Hiring remarkable team members is just as much about spotting the wannabes as it is about spotting the champions. One of our remark-*ability* trainers at ReviewBuzz suggests that you extend the "hiring" process into the training period by shadowing your new hires. Within one week, you'll know whether someone has the potential for being remark-*able*. It will be obvious not just in what they do in response to customer requests and customer complaints it will also be obvious in *how* they do it.

Customers aren't fools, they can tell when you're just doing something because it's your job or when you truly have a commitment to customer satisfaction in your blood. This isn't always obvious during the interview process, but give the person a week or two in a customer service position and you'll know whether you've got a champ or a chump.

Tony Hsieh of Zappos has a habit of hiring people directly into customer service positions from the very beginning. It didn't matter if they were the CFO, COO or the guy who emptied out the trash bin on the seventh floor.

If they were employed by Tony Hsieh, they had a two-week tour of the world of the Zappos customer service experience. He did this to see if he wanted them to work for his company long term. After the first week of training and continuing through the four-week process, Zappos offered the new hires $2,000 to quit the company. If they said yes and took the check, Tony Hsieh just paid two thousand dollars to discover he didn't want that person working for his company.

It might be easy to think the cheese had fallen out of this Tony's sandwich. Why in the world would you spend $2k to get *rid* of someone who you'd just spent two weeks training? Tony did this because he wanted people working for him who saw the value in being a customer service superstar at a place like Zappos. If they were willing to give up a guaranteed $2,000 in order to stay at the company, he knew he had someone who "got it."

Ever heard of the saying, *"You can't fly like an eagle if you're surrounded by Turkeys?"*

Here's my version: *"You can't have a Goose that lays golden eggs if you're surrounding him with rotten eggs."*

If you want your business to become remarkable, make it a number one priority to ask yourself this question when it comes to hiring and training new team members: *"Does this person have the Golden Goose DNA?"*

TARGETED **TIPS**

HIRING TIP: When hiring and training new team members ask yourself, "Does this person have the Golden Goose DNA?"

If you have your doubts, don't risk it. There are too many people out of work these days for you to settle for the first warm body that comes along. Hold out for someone who has the Golden Goose DNA, it will be worth it.

Earlier in this book I referenced Jim Collins, author of Good to Great. Jim's research is worth revisiting again. He found that of the fastest growing businesses in the United States, the best performing companies were those which focused on having the right people "on the bus." This was their number one priority, even before growing the business. I'd also like to remind you that Google started out with a 10-interview process for determining whether they wanted to hire someone to work for their company.

## Who's in Charge of the Buzz?

Do you have a Chief Buzz Officer (CBO) in your organization? Someone in charge of being proactive about creating and maintaining a buzz-worthy company image online? Here's why that position is so important.

The first thing on the CBO's agenda is checking out the company's online reputation. What do potential customers see when they look up your company's name or local companies in your industry? How can your company generate more positive reviews? Are reviews properly representing your company's true reputation online?

Your CBO needs to focus on your company reviews as an external element of your reputation, and they also need to focus on the internal personnel representing and generating that reputation. Your team needs to understand that every service call is a potential good or bad review, therefore being great is no longer a bonus, it's a company non-negotiable.

Lastly, the CBO should work within the company to share positive public reviews with the remark-*able* teams. That might mean working with your HR department or an employment manager. Not only do potential new customers need to be assured that you are a top-rated

For convenience, a list of roles & job descriptions mentioned here can be found at: SMBRbook.com/roles

business, the same goes for quality employee prospects. Establishing your company as an employer of choice means you have the benefit of choosing from the best potential candidates. Besides who doesn't like to be appreciated? If management recognizes 5-star customer service achievements then the rest of the team will naturally begin competing.

It must become part of your operational initiatives to incorporate a review and feedback segment into weekly meetings. Implement a reward system for tracking and delivering customer service "commissions" and for making sure your top service stars get the recognition they need and deserve.

Your CBO and the appropriate managers should continuously coach and measure all teams to assure everyone is blowing their customers away with an extraordinary experience. Having this kind of team in place will help you create an invaluable customer experience. But most importantly, you need to get the person in the driver's seat *obsessed* with transforming your company into a remarkable company.

## Communication and Training: The Language of Being Remarkable

For everything you can now do well, there was a time when you were terrible at it.

It's the same thing for winning reviews. The beginning won't be a walk in the park. It will take twisting some employee's arms, pushing them out of their comfort zones, and conducting meetings. It will also require brainstorming sessions about how to track and monitor the performance of your team members and how to reward your best performers.

There is a learning curve for the people of your organization to start speaking the language of being remarkable. Some of our customers at ReviewBuzz hit the ground running and get 30 reviews in the first 60 days while others take more time to get traction.

There's one thing you'll need in order to make sure the new culture of remarkability gets *traction* with your organization. You'll need solid and consistent communication and training about the process of *winning* reviews, not just asking for reviews, but earning them. But don't forget to emphasize that the review is the reward for remarkable service. The focus of your training should always be service first, reviews second.

This is a small distinction, but it's a crucial one, especially when it comes to training your employees to build a remarkable buzz-worthy company. If you tell your employees to start asking for reviews, they'll start doing just that, *asking*. You can even tell them you'll reward them for getting reviews. You can threaten to fire them for not asking. But if all they do is ask for reviews, they won't get them. They won't follow the ABCs of being remarkable and because of this they won't get many, if any reviews. After a while, the chore of asking will become just one more reason for them to throw darts at your picture in the break room. Not to mention that by solely asking for a review you'll irritate the customers who didn't receive remark-*able* service in the first place.

If you get all the steps in this process right, asking for the review should be just as easy as asking the customer to write you a check for your services. However, it has to be a step-by-step process and that's why training plays a critical role in creating a remarkable company culture.

# Rev Up Your Reps with Review Rallies

The best training mixes rewards and recognition in with the training itself. Most companies call these training meetings "sales rallies." I recommend that companies also have Review Rallies.

At a Review Rally, you talk about winning reviews instead of making sales. You reward the people who won the most reviews and you have them share how they did it.

By now you know how powerful reviews are when it comes to making sales, so focusing on earning reviews *and* making sales will just increase your company sales all the more. In fact, because reviews and sales go hand in hand I suggest you have review training, Review Rallies, sales training *and* sales rallies. The increase in your bottom line, your company growth, the improvement in your company culture and the increase in employee retention and satisfaction will more than make up for the extra time spent.

During the time while I was writing this book, one of our customers, Craig Denton from Anton's Heating and Cooling, told me about a Review Rally he had at his company. This wasn't your typical company "get together and pat each other on the back" meeting. It was a cross between a sales meeting, a family barbecue and a charismatic church service. Craig set the goal for his team of winning 30 reviews in 60 days. The purpose of the review rally was to celebrate accomplishing that goal.

Here are just a few things he did at this Review Rally.
1. Arranged a catered dinner
2. Had contests and prizes
3. Read customer feedback and reviews aloud to everyone
4. Invited his employee's spouses and family members

**POWER** TIPS
*Secret Training Formula:*

Sales Training
Review Training
Sales Rallies
**+** Review Rallies

Remark-*able* Company Culture

When the reviews were read aloud, things "got real." People were actually holding back tears, hugging one another and some of them said they left the rally a different person than when they walked in. It gives me goose bumps just writing about it.

The employees were also awarded raffle tickets according to how many reviews they earned. There were contests where people could spin the wheel and win cash prizes. The grand prize was a flat screen HD TV, and we're not talking a little one that sits on your kitchen table. Craig was standing by the wheel as the employees were spinning it and cheering, "Break the bank, break the bank!"

How different is that from what a lot of business owners are doing right now? They're making cut backs and laying people off, in fear that the *state of the economy* will break the bank. That reminds me of a well-known quote by Steve Jobs at the time the recession first started and companies were laying off people.

*"A lot of companies have chosen to downsize, and maybe that was the right thing for them. We chose a different path. Our belief was that if we kept putting great products in front of customers, they would continue to open their wallets." - Steve Jobs*

By now, you should know that Steve Jobs wasn't just talking about selling iPads, iPhones and lap tops. The most valuable products you have to offer at your company are your employee-to-customer interactions. If you break the bank investing in building remarkable employees, your customers will continue to open their wallets too.

When was the last time your company held a sales meeting that someone would describe as a positive, life-changing, emotionally beneficial experience? If you want to win one hundred percent of your team members' efforts when it comes to creating a culture of remarkability, start holding Review Rallies.

## Who Are Your Key Players?

Becoming remarkable is a team effort, and you'll need to get traction within your company by starting with the leaders and the key influencers. This starts with identifying your key players such as your managers, team leaders, and front line personnel. Of course, not everyone will hit the ground running. In every organization, you have people who catch on quickly and pioneer change, and you have people who dig their heels in thinking it's just another stuffy company policy.

Start with your influencers, first your managers and then your team leaders. Find the most influential front line personnel and focus most of your energy on getting them bought into the philosophy of winning reviews. If you direct your energy on the key  influencers, you'll affect change a lot faster than you would focusing on the reluctant staff members. The most important person to get one hundred percent buy-in from, both in beliefs and actions, is you. We'll talk more about that in just a moment.

So what does it take to get your key people on board with your new venture to create a remarkable company? You'll need five things:

1. Clear expectations: make it clear exactly what you expect them to do to earn reviews.
2. Examples: proof of other people and companies who have created success by winning reviews (feel free to use any of the real-life examples in this book).
3. Accountability: reviews will be a great way to manage and measure their performance and keep them accountable to improve it.
4. Rewards: people work much better when you give them recognition and incentives.
5. Resources: make it clear what resources are available for helping them succeed.

## Accountability: Challenging People to Do Their Best

Accountability is a must for building a remarkable organization.

Right now, there is untapped potential within your organization. I guarantee it. If you want to find out where it is and just how much potential is available, you need accountability. No matter how self-motivated someone is, they'll always do better when they know that they'll be held to a high standard. In fact, even people who resist accountability at first secretly want it. They want to realize their potential, to be challenged and to become more. Many of them are just waiting for the right opportunity to make it happen.

YOU can bring them this opportunity, and if you do this in conjunction with the other rules in this chapter, you'll be amazed before you're halfway into it.

The funny thing about accountability is that it's normally seen as a negative thing at first, even by the people who come to welcome it later. It's only after people begin to discover the power that accountability has to help them reach their full potential that they embrace it.

"If you can't measure it, you can't manage it."

– Peter Drucker

For example, at 1-800-Anytyme our customer service representatives were not capturing email addresses when they spoke to potential and new customers. It was important to have this information to successful connect with the customer before and after the service call to demonstrate and improve our remarkable service.

Even with thorough training and reminders, our email collection percentage was very low. That's when I created a tracking system that could measure performance and make the staff accountable for their own results. I installed and consistently utilized a scoreboard that was out in the open for everyone to see their success, or their areas of opportunities to improve. By keeping score, this one method created immediate, dramatic improvements. The purpose was not to humiliate anyone but to make it very obvious how well everyone was doing, which lead to the inevitable congratulations and personal pride. As the normal course of human behavior would dictate, it also led to a little healthy competition among the staff to pushed themselves to do better than their previous numbers and better than their colleagues.

As the leader of your organization, it's your job to create a culture of discipline and accountability, even if you're met with some initial resistance. Your team members WILL thank you for it in the long run. They'll begin to do and accomplish things they always suspected they were capable of, but which they never pushed themselves hard enough to achieve.

That's a very empowering feeling, and it's one which can only be reached through challenging people to push past their limits. I recently read Charles M. Province's book, *Patton's One-Minute Messages* (Presidio Press, 1995) about General Patton where he talked about the power of expectations and how it's impossible to become great without it.

Here's what he said:

"When you're put in charge – whether it's of an army, division, battalion, company, platoon or special detail –
**ACT LIKE YOU'RE IN CHARGE.**

Make damn sure you're in control at all times and that you know what's going on. Ninety percent of being in command is nothing more than making sure orders are followed and the mission accomplished.

**ONCE YOU'VE ISSUED AN ORDER, GET THE HELL OUT OF THE WAY OF THE PEOPLE DOING THE JOB,**

but make sure they know you're in charge, that you expect them to bring the mission to full fruition, and that they are responsible for its completion."

**- General George Patton**

This is true in any organization or any discipline. That's why some of the world's greatest athletes still work with coaches. The worlds' greatest musicians still meet with teachers on a consistent basis and the best dancers still work with trainers. Heck, even the Olympic champions have coaches. They don't stop training or stop having someone hold them accountable to be their best because they "no longer need it."

They can't afford to do that because they've made a personal commitment to be remarkable. It's the same thing with your organization. You and your team members need clear standards, to be reminded of those standards and to be held accountable to them. Without this, even the most self-motivated person will become relaxed and switch out of fifth gear and back into third or fourth.

But the most important reason you need accountability is to find out where the missing potential exists. This is where customer feedback can really come to your aid, and I'm not just talking about reviews. At ReviewBuzz, we started out just helping companies get positive reviews posted in the online marketplace.

This is more than most companies are doing, but there's a whole other level of commitment to becoming remark-*able* which is based not on gathering reviews, but on gathering feedback from customers. Not every customer will write a review, either because the service provider did not earn it, or because the customer simply did not want to write a public recommendation. In those two scenarios, it is crucial to survey the customers. The most important question when conducting a survey is this:

*"On a scale of 0-10, how likely is it that you would recommend our service to a friend?"*

The customer is asked to answer this question based on a 0-10 scale, ten being the most likely to recommend and zero being a "no way would I ever recommend this company." Here's how the results of such a question break down:

- An answer of 0-6 is considered a detractor (Ranter). This is someone who is likely to say not-so-nice things about your company.
- An answer of 7 or 8 is considered a Passive. This is someone who isn't likely to say anything about your company, good or bad.
- An answer of 9 or 10 means they will recommend your company to others.

Now, take the total amount of promoters, subtract the number of detractors and you've got something called your "Net Promoter Score" (NPS). This is a tangible, measurable way to unveil the mystery of why you might be struggling for repeat customers. The NPS is a real and measurable metric used by companies like:

- JetBlue Airways

- Four Seasons

- Southwest Airlines

- Zappos

- UnderArmour

- American Express

(For more information on how to use surveys to increase reviews go to www.SMBRbook.com/nps)

## Recognition Power: Lead With the Carrot, Not the Stick

Anyone who has managed employees or raised children knows you need incentives to motivate people. Here are just a few of the statistics proving the power of incentives in raising a company's profits:

- 69% of workers surveyed say that non-monetary forms of recognition provide the best motivation. (Source: *The Gallup Organization, Marketing Magazine*, May 2007)

- Companies with high levels of employee engagement ... improved their operating income by 19.2% ... while companies with low levels of engagement saw their operating income decline by 32.7% over a 12 month period. (Source: "FORUM — The Economic Case for People Performance Management and Measurement," December 2007)

- Companies that reward their employees for being innovative increase their revenues by 2.5% and their profit margins by 2%. (Source: IBM Global Business Consulting CEO Survey, December 2006)

Notice that these statistics don't mention anything about customer reviews, but you'd better believe if you can raise your profits and revenues using employee rewards, you can also create a more remarkable customer service experience and thus raise the number of positive reviews your company has online.

You've probably been to at least one place of business where you had a bad customer service experience because the person working behind the counter was pouting about how unhappy they were with their job. Sometimes, the worker is just an unhappy person, but even happy and ambitious employees can be reduced to a long-faced, poker-playing dog if they feel unappreciated by their employer.

If you want to keep your team members motivated about creating remarkable experiences for your customers, you need incentives. Of course, a self-motivated person will work without incentives for a while because they take pride in doing good work. That, in conjunction with a steady paycheck is enough to keep them going....for a while. But everyone has their limits, and even the most self-motivated person will burn out in time if they're not earning the right types of incentives.

On the other hand, you've probably found that self-motivated people are fairly hard to come by. Even if you get a few of them working for your company, the majority of your team may still be people who require external motivation. Your job as the company leader is to fuel and magnify the drive of your naturally self-motivated team members and *keep their motivation alive. You must do this in addition to* providing the proper external motivation for your other team members.

You do this with incentives, and the practice of winning positive customer reviews creates the perfect environment for using incentives to motivate your team. I say this because a positive review itself provides the irresistible incentive of recognition from your customers. Yes, money definitely motivates people, and I do suggest you have contests where team members with the most reviews can win prizes and other perks. To do this you'll need a method of tracking who earned what review from what customer. A tracking system will serve three purposes.

- Help you easily track and reward your most efficient review earners.
- Help you to discover who is lagging behind in earning reviews.
- Connecting a team member to each review will give them a rock solid validation that their efforts are being genuinely recognized and appreciated.

ReviewBuzz is a review tracking system is that allows the customer to connect their positive review to the salesperson, customer service agent, or team of individuals, who assisted the customer and thus earned the review. Personalized reviews are like a bazooka of strategy when it comes to breaking down your team members' inhibitions about giving remarkable service.

Many people work harder to get recognition than they do to earn extra money or prizes. Don't get me wrong, you can't just give people a "Coke and a Smile" and pay them barely enough to make rent, groceries and their Netflix fee every month. You should still reward your most remarkable review earners using monetary incentives. But never underestimate the power of recognition. It addresses one of the deepest and most powerful human needs — the need for validation and approval. Most importantly, never underestimate the power of surveying your customer's experience when deciding who to reward and to recognize for their contribution to creating a remarkable company. If you have representatives who aren't stacking up the reviews, but who are helping you up your NPS score, reward them for it.

The more you do this, the more natural it will be to become remark-*able*. Here are some raw statistics of how real employees feel about the power of recognition:

• A survey of over 2,000 workers has found that 80% of employees said praise and recognition motivates them to do a better job. (Source: Gallup, August 2006)

• 74% of employees say being recognized by their managers for doing good work is very or extremely important. (Source: Nielson, June 2006)

People will leave jobs where they feel unappreciated, even if they're making a lot of money. I know a guy who was working for a large communications company making over $100k a year who took a pay cut and left because of the way he was being treated by his team and managers.

This might sound crazy to an outsider because it might be easy to say you'd "stick it out just for the money." But put even the most money-motivated person in that situation long enough and the drain on their emotional wellbeing will wear them down like a gourmet chef being forced to eat a diet of plain oatmeal for a solid year.

People are naturally wired to connect with other people and seek recognition and acceptance, it's a survival instinct. So never assume that offering a paycheck alone is enough to incentivize them and convince them to help your company become remarkable.

However, if you put someone in a culture where they can earn acceptance and recognition *and* earn a decent living, they'll become a remarkable and loyal employee. This is the foundation of building a great company culture. It starts with instilling the components of a remarkable culture into the "citizens" of your organization.

Trying to build a remarkable company culture without incentivizing your employee is like trying to build a solid house out of straw. Great companies are built upon great employees, so you need to make sure your company is a breeding ground for creating employees who go above and beyond to deliver exceptional service. You get out of people what you invest in them, and being remarkable is contagious. Create a remarkable experience for your employees and they'll do the same for your customers. Everybody wins.

# What about Your "Unmotivated" Employees?

Think you have someone working for you who won't respond to or appreciate incentives? Don't assume, just try them out and see for yourself the true power of the incentive. In the documentary movie, *Freakonomics*, one of the economists tells a story about how he helped a little girl become potty trained.

Just to give you an idea of what this guy was up against, the little girl's mother had read several books and spent many sleepless nights pouring over potty-training websites. Nevertheless, her daughter was busy writing her own potty literature all over the house: "Yellow Rivers are Flowing'" by: I.P Freely.

Then, an economist stepped in claiming that with the right incentive he could get anyone to do just about anything. He started offering the little girl Skittles™ candies for every time she went potty in the right place. That put a dam in the yellow rivers and accomplished what the mother wasn't able to accomplish by pouring over books on potty training. The little girl had 100 percent success rate and even became excited about going to the restroom. It probably took years

for her to realize the actual benefit of going potty in the toilet (and she probably developed diabetes in the meantime), but the Skittles™ provided a set of "training wheels" to keep her motivated until she realized the genuine benefit for herself.

It's the same thing with those employees who you assume won't see the value of winning customer reviews. Providing them with incentives will get them doing it for the sake of winning the incentives. After a time, they'll see the positive impact on their relationship with their customers and their managers. They'll start to realize that more positive reviews means more business and more job security.

They'll eventually conclude that working for your company is better than working for the competition because of the remarkable reputation you've worked to build. They'll start to "get it," but if they can't see that bigger picture at first, you have to start with where they are right now. You have to start by dangling the carrot of incentives.

Do this right, and you won't need to threaten your employees or nag them about "getting their act together." In my experience working with hundreds of customers, I've seen some of the best sales reps go from not "getting it" when it came to winning reviews to becoming some of the best review champs at their company.

I specifically remember one salesperson I'll call "Mark." Mark wasn't known for his customer satisfaction skills. In fact, I was told he was sometimes rude to customers when things didn't go his way. Mark was approached by his boss and advised he would be terminated if he didn't stop being rude to the customers. Yet it just seemed to not be Mark's nature to treat customers well. Then, during one of the company "Review Rallies," Mark realized that the less-talented sales people were starting to *outsell him* because they were better at earning reviews. They were winning the sales contests and being entered into drawings for flat screen TVs, movie tickets and gift certificates while he was sitting by like a kid banished to time-out at a birthday party. That did it. His competitive nature kicked in and he got his butt in gear. Once he realized reviews could help him get more sales, he became one of the top review earners at his company.

Within just a few weeks, he was back on top of the game and winning more reviews than anyone else. Finally, Mark started to realize the recognition had its own rewards and that creating a remarkable customer service experience was just as much a part of the sales process as closing and overcoming objections. He was motivated by growing his revenue and if reviews were the way to get there, he would make them work for him, and in turn he provided better service for the customer. Now that's a chain reaction worth repeating. For Mark, it took using incentives to get him to that point. I encourage you to do the same thing if you want your team members to understand and engage the philosophy of becoming remark-*able*.

If you keep trying to persuade them with threats, punishments, and long-winded speeches and meetings on the value of being remarkable, you'll probably always have at least a few people who don't "get it."

Incentives are more than just a tool for motivating your team members. They're also a powerful educational tool. They provide the validation that winning customer reviews have a direct positive benefit. The positive benefits we've been talking about in this book might not be as easily and immediately noticeable to your team members. Incentives, on the other hand, are easily and immediately noticeable. If you want to get your company to the promised land of being remarkable, start with the dangling carrot of incentives.

## Leadership and the Remarkable Obsession with Customer Service

As a closing invitation, I invite you to awaken an obsession; an obsession with creating a remarkable experience. Not just for your customers, but for your managers, your team leaders, your front line personnel and most important for yourself.

From the moment you put down this book, you can be having the time of your life running and growing your company, squashing your competition and changing what's possible for yourself and the people who work for you.

The secret to making this happen, and the most remarkable secret to growing your company, is to get one hundred percent focused on delivering a remarkable customer experience. Once you spread this thought process throughout your organization you'll build an unstoppable momentum that will carry your company up and up and up. It all starts here, so get obsessed.

*Being remarkable starts with remarkable* **leadership**.

We are in the age of the empowered customer. No longer can customer service take a back seat to marketing, accounting, annual reports and endless company meetings. Once you start to focus on making a positive customer experience your top priority and something your entire company embraces, customers will be excited to share and your good reputation will spread across review sites, online directories and Social Media sites.

UGC, Social Media, SEO, Pay Per Click, direct mail, digital word-of-mouth marketing, customer service training, Review Rallies…you name it. The success of all those strategies will rise and fall on the shoulders of *your* leadership. Who will *you* be to your customers and your team members? What kind of example will you set?

I want you to picture the CEO of a billion dollar company sitting, not in a corner office overlooking the city skyline, but sitting in a sea of cubicles, amidst his customer service team. Now I want you to picture the CEO of the wealthiest company in the United States, one of the greatest minds of his time, sitting at his laptop responding to customer service emails.

The two CEOs I'm talking about are Tony Hsieh of Zappos and the late Steve Jobs of Apple. Tony Hsieh put his office directly in the middle of the "sea of cubicles" so that he could know exactly what was happening with his front line personnel. How different would your company run if you made this kind of shift in priority?

Then there's Steve Jobs, who everyone thought grew Apple into the most successful business in the United States simply by creating great technology. I'm sure that had a lot to do with it, but hardly anyone knows about or talks about Steve Jobs' obsession with great customer service with his "hands on" involvement in co-writing the customer service manuals for the Apple stores.

There have been many companies who have come out with great technologies over the years, including Apple's biggest competitor Microsoft. Microsoft isn't really known for their customer service, and as social media has become more and more influential in driving people's buying decisions, Apple has used this to their advantage.

As we progress further into the age of digital word-of-mouth marketing, the customer service focused CEO will slowly drive the CEO who sits in a high tower of solitude, counting money all day, into extinction. Clever product innovations won't stand a chance unless the creator of those products knows how to take care of customer relationships.

In the age of digital word-of-mouth marketing, great leadership starts with an obsession with customer service. We-we marketing as a stand-alone is dead. It won't convince your customers of the value of doing business with you and it certainly won't convince your managers, team leaders and team members to make remarkable service a priority.

The age of social media demands authenticity and transparency. There is no "fake it 'till you make it" when it comes to being remarkable. If you want to make it in the new economy, you have to sincerely put customers first, and if you don't, you'll be last.

The word is out. People are talking, and they're out to lift up remarkable people and companies.

You can't wait any longer to take action when it comes to remark-ability and online reviews. It's here now and if you don't get started, you will be left in the dust. Google is already preparing you for the power of the review so you had better pay attention and start integrating the strategies in this book into your organization. But remember, don't lead with the review. Don't think of the reviews as just one more thing in your marketing bucket.

This is not about marketing it's about being remark-*able*. Managing measureable results and integrating transparent reward systems will earn you not only 5-star employees, but 5-star reviews. Let's face it, when your customer's experience is buzz-worthy, all other areas of your organization benefit.

It's up to *you* to lead your company in the right direction, starting *right now*.

# Chapter Six Summary:

1. If you put someone in a culture where they can earn acceptance and recognition *and* earn a decent living, they'll become a remarkable and loyal employee. This is the foundation of building a remarkable company culture.

2. You'll need solid and consistent communication and training about the process of *winning* reviews, not just asking for reviews, but *winning* reviews.

3. If you get all the steps in this process right, asking for the review should be just as easy as asking the customer to write you a check for your services. However, it has to be a step-by-step process and that's why training plays a big role in creating a remarkable company culture.

4. Find the most influential front line personnel and focus most of your energy on getting their buy-in to the philosophy of winning reviews.

5. When there's more accountability to provide great service *and* a new level of confidence that the great service will be rewarded and recognized, you will get 100 percent of someone's effort.

6. Your business must assign someone who can monitor daily and weekly activity about review generation and whose job it is to motivate the team

to stay active in becoming and remaining buzz-worthy through remarkable customer service and a commitment to soliciting positive reviews.

7. Take action today — go out and make your company remarkable!

# Chapter 6 Recommended Reading

*Freakonomics: A Rogue Economist Explores the Hidden Side of Everything*, Steven D. Levitt and Stephen J. Dubner (William Morrow Paperback, 2009)

*The Carrot Principle: How the Best Managers Use Recognition to Engage Their People, Retain Talent, and Accelerate Performance* [Updated & Revised], Adrian Gostick and Chester Elton (Free Press, 2009)

*The Zappos Experience: 5 Principles to Inspire, Engage, and WOW,* Joseph A. Michelli (McGraw-Hill, 2011)

*Tribal Leadership: Leveraging Natural Groups to Build a Thriving Organization*, Dave Logan, John King and Halee Fischer-Wright (HarperBusiness, 2011)

*Tribes: We Need You to Lead Us*, Seth Godin (Portfolio Hardcover, 2008)

*Who: The A Method for Hiring,* Geoff Smart and Randy Street (Ballantine Books, 2008)

For convenience, a list of tools provided by ReviewBuzz.com can be found at: **SMBRbook.com/reviewbuzz**

.

# LISTED RESOURCES

## Acknowledgement:

*Unleash the Power Within, Tony Robbins*
*http://www.tonyrobbins.com/events/unleash-the-power-within*

## Introduction:

*Landing Page Optimization: The Definitive Guide to Testing and Tuning for Conversions, Tim Ash (Wiley Press, 2008)*

## Chapter 1:

*Trust Agents: Using the Web to Build Influence, Improve Reputation, and Earn Trust,* Chris Brogan and Julian Smith (Wiley Press, 2010)

"Are Online Reviews More Influential Than Advertising, " Colette Bennett (SearchInfluence.com, 02/07/2012) http://www.searchinfluence.com/2012/02/online-reviews-advertising-influence/

*AKA (Deloitte & Touche, 2007)*

https://quantcast.com/

*Social BOOM!: How to Master Business Social Media to Brand Yourself, Sell Yourself, Sell Your Product, Dominate Your Industry Market, Save Your Butt, ... and Grind Your Competition into the Dirt,* Jeffrey Gitomer (FT Press, 2011)

*The Seven Habits of Highly Effective People,* Stephen Covey (Free Press, 2004)

http://dankennedy.com

"New JCP Company Goes Back To Origins To Find Its Future," Patrick Hanlon (Forbes.com, 3/03/2012)

http://www.forbes.com/sites/patrickhanlon/2012/03/03/new-jcp-company-goes-back-to-origins-to-find-its-future/

## Chapter 2:

"Google's Trusted Stores,"

http://www.google.com/trustedstores/merchants/

"Loud Commercials," FCC Media Bureau (FCC.gov, 03/07/2011) http://www.fcc.gov/encyclopedia/loud-commercials

"Online Influence Trend Tracker," (Cone Communications, 2011)
http://www.conecomm.com/2011coneonlineinfluencetrendtracker

"The Death of SEO: The Rise of Social, PR, and Real Content," Ken Krogue (Forbes.com, 07/20/12)

http://www.forbes.com/sites/kenkrogue/2012/07/20/the-death-of-seo-the-rise-of-social-pr-and-real-content/

"For The First Time Ever, Smartphones Outsold PCs Last Quarter," Matt Rosoff (BusinessInsider.com, 02/03/12)

http://articles.businessinsider.com/2012-02-03/tech/31020138_1_pc-sales-tablet-sales-smartphone#ixzz277hxsgcR

## Chapter 3:

"How Social Media Is Changing Customer Service," Michael Vizard (ITBusinessEdge.com, 07/14/2011)

http://www.itbusinessedge.com/cm/blogs/vizard/how-social-media-is-changing-customer-service/?cs=47819

*The Zappos Experience: 5 Principles to Inspire, Engage, and WOW*, Joseph A. Michelli (McGraw-Hill, 2011)

"Nordstrom Customer Service Catalyzes Growth" Cotton Timberlake (Bloomberg BusinessWeek, August 14th, 2011)

http://www.sfgate.com/business/article/Nordstrom-s-customer-service-catalyzes-growth-2334880.php

*Letters to Steve: Inside the E-mail Inbox of Apple's Steve Jobs,* Mark Milian (Kindle Edition, 11/ 21/2011).

"Apple's Customer Service Secrets Revealed: A.P.P.L.E." Andy Hanselman (Socialmediatoday.com, 07/16/2011) http://socialmediatoday.com/andyhanselman/551259/apple-s-customer-service-secrets-revealed-apple

"Secrets from Apple's Genuis Bar: Full Loyalty, No Negativity," Yukari Iwatani Kane and Ian Sherr (Wall

Street Journal, 06/15/2011)
http://online.wsj.com/article/SB10001424052702304563104576364071955678908.html
*Delivering Happiness.* Tony Hsieh. (Business Plus,

06/07/2010)

*Multiple Streams of Income*, Robert G. Allen (Wiley Press

04/05/05)

*The Seven Habits of Highly Effective People,* Stephen
Covey (Free Press, 11/09/04)

"EXPO Communications Report" (ComScore, 2011)

http://www.comscore.com/


## CHAPTER 4

"88% of consumers consult reviews when making a
purchase," David Moth (Econsultancy.com, May 22, 2012)

http://econsultancy.com/us/blog/9958-88-of-consumers-consult-reviews-when-making-a-purchase

*Good to Great: Why Some Companies Make the Leap...
and Others Don't*, Jim Collins (HarperBusiness 10/16/01)

Social Network Feedback Sparks Tempur-Pedic's Sales,
(Investors.com, 02/04/11)
http://news.investors.com/article/562136/201102041545/social-network-feedback-sparks-tempur-pedics-sales.htm?p=full

*Scarface,* Universal Pictures, 1983

## Chapter 5

"Google Places Policies and Guidelines"
http://support.google.com/places/bin/answer.py?hl=en&ans
wer=187622

"New Google Algorithm to Punish Bad Businesses" (
Xmotion.co.uk , 12/08/2011)
http://www.xtmotion.co.uk/new-google-algorithm-to-
punish-bad-businesses/

"Firm to Pay FTC $250, 000 to Settle Charges That It
Used Misleading Online "Consumer" and "Independent"
Reviews," (FTC.gov, 03/15/2011)

http://ftc.gov/opa/2011/03/legacy.shtm

*The Social Network Movie,* Relativity Media, 2010.

*Cornell Software Fingers Fake Online Reviews,* Eric
Smalley (CNET, 07/26/2011)

*Finding Deceptive Opinion Spam by Any Stretch of the
Imagination,* Claire Cardie, Choi Yejin, Jeffrey T. Hancock
and Myle Ott (Cornell University, 07/22/2011)
http://aclweb.org/anthology-new/P/P11/P11-1032.pdf

"Google Adds More Of Its Own Goodies To Search
Results, Despite Antitrust Concerns" (The Huffington Post,
11/02/2011)

http://www.huffingtonpost.com/2011/11/02/google-adds-
search-features_n_1071323.html

"The Fireworks Restoration Company, LLC vs. Michael Hosto," *The Missouri Court of Appeals Eastern District Court Transcript* (05/09/2012) http://digitalcommons.law.scu.edu/cgi/viewcontent.cgi?article=1071&context=historical

ReviewBuzz.com/ezReview

## Chapter 6:

*Good to Great: Why Some Companies Make the Leap... and Others Don't,* Jim Collins (HarperBusiness, 10/16/2001)

*Patton's One-Minute Messages,* Charles M. Province (Presidio Press, 1995)

"The Net Promoter Score and System," (Satmetrix)

http://www.netpromoter.com/why-net-promoter/know/

The Gallup Organization, *Marketing Magazine*, (May 2007) http://www.motive8.com.au/incentive_statistics

"FORUM — The Economic Case for People Performance Management and Measurement," (December 2007)

http://www.motive8.com.au/incentive_statistics

IBM Global Business Consulting CEO Survey, (December 2006) http://www.motive8.com.au/incentive_statistics

Gallup, August 2006.

http://www.motive8.com.au/incentive_statistics

Nielson, June 2006.

http://www.motive8.com.au/incentive_statistics\

*Freakonomics*, Magnolia Pictures, 2010.

# Recommended Resources

- Review Power Blog

www.reviewpower.com

- Call Source

http://callsource.com/

- Ellen Rohr – Bare Bones Biz

www.barebonesbiz.com

- Legal Zoom

www.LegalZoom.com

- Rocket Lawyers

www.RocketLawyer.com

- Hub Spot

www.Hubspot.com

- ZapposInsights

www.Zapposinsights.com

- GTD Connect

https://secure.davidco.com/connect/

- BaseCamp

http://Basecamphq.com

- Freshbooks

www.Freshbooks.com

- Mint

www.Mint.com

- Hootsuite - http://hootsuite.com/
- *Freakonomics*. Dir. Alex Gibney and Eugene Jarecki. 2010. DVD. Magnolia Pictures, 2011.

## Recommended Reading

*Crush It!: Why NOW Is the Time to Cash In on Your Passion*, Gary Vaynerchuk (Harper Studio, 2009)

*Delivering Happiness: A Path to Profits, Passion, and Purpose*, Tony Hsieh (Business Plus, 2010)

*Freakonomics: A Rogue Economist Explores the Hidden Side of Everything*, Steven D. Levitt and Stephen J. Dubner (William Morrow Paperback, 2009)

*Good to Great: Why Some Companies Make the Leap... and Others Don't*, Jim Collins (HarperBusiness, 2001)

*"I Love You More Than My Dog": Five Decisions That Drive Extreme Customer Loyalty in Good Times and Bad*, Jeanne Bliss (Portfolio Trade, 2011)

*Landing Page Optimization: The Definitive Guide to Testing and Tuning for Conversions*, Tim Ash (Sybex, 2008)

*Social BOOM!: How to Master Business Social Media to Brand Yourself, Sell Yourself, Sell Your Product, Dominate Your Industry Market, Save Your Butt, ... and Grind Your Competition into the Dirt*, Jeffrey H. Gitomer (FT Press, 2011)

*The Carrot Principle: How the Best Managers Use Recognition to Engage Their People, Retain Talent, and Accelerate*

*Performance* [Updated & Revised], Adrian Gostick and Chester Elton (Free Press, 2009)

*The SPEED of Trust: The One Thing That Changes Everything*, Stephen M.R. Covey (Free Press, 2008)

*The Zappos Experience: 5 Principles to Inspire, Engage, and WOW,* Joseph A. Michelli (McGraw-Hill, 2011)

*The Ultimate Question 2.0 (Revised and Expanded Edition): How Net Promoter Companies Thrive in a Customer-Driven World,* Fred Reichheld and Rob Markey (Harvard Business Review Press, 2011)

*Tribal Leadership: Leveraging Natural Groups to Build a Thriving Organization*, Dave Logan, John King and Halee Fischer-Wright (HarperBusiness, 2011)

*Tribes: We Need You to Lead Us*, Seth Godin (Portfolio Hardcover, 2008)

*Trust Agents: Using the Web to Build Influence, Improve Reputation, and Earn Trust,* Chris Brogan and Julien Smith (Wiley, 2010)

*Who: The A Method for Hiring,* Geoff Smart and Randy Street (Ballantine Books, 2008)

*Word of Mouth Marketing*: *How Smart Companies Get People Talking,* Andy Sernovitz (Greenleaf Book Group Press, 2012)

*Winning the Zero Moment of Truth – ZMOT,* Jim Lecinski (Vook, 2011)